PRAISE FOR *YOUR FAMILY CONSTITUTION*

"*Your Family Constitution* is a witty and insightful journey of self discovery and parental understanding! This book will alter parents' attitudes and expectations, while guiding the way toward progressive improvement in family disposition and circumstance. *Your Family Constitution* is essential reading for parents interested in preserving the mental health of their children, as well as their own."

—PETER R. WELGAN, PH.D., CLINICAL PSYCHOLOGIST

"A practical new look at how to improve family relationships from the 'ground up.' Written from the perspective of a husband and father who recognized a better way, Scott Gale has created a blueprint families can follow to open lines of communication, affirm personal values, and assure improved life skills for the long term...while having fun together. It's a real winner!"

—SANDRA L. GARRISON, SCHOOL PSYCHOLOGIST

"Today, youth struggle with a multitude of issues, including entitlement, isolation, and most of all, lack of direction. Fortunately, parents can redirect their children by creating boundaries and managing their children's expectations. *Your Family Constitution* enables parents to implement such a plan, simply and effectively."

—MELISSA A. GIBSON, SCHOOL COUNSELOR, M.F.T.I.

"Scott Gale has found a way to make family life easier and more fun for parents and kids alike. As a teacher and observer of the new generation of kids, I know that parents today need this tool more than ever before. I gave this book to my daughters in hopes that my grandchildren will grow up to reflect the family values with which I raised my kids."

—JACKIE DILLON, HIGH SCHOOL TEACHER

MORE PRAISE

"This is by far the best book on household structure I've seen...The best part of the book is that he doesn't just tell you WHAT to do, he tells you how he did it, why he did it, and what happened when he tried to put it in place."

—SMS BOOK REVIEWS

★ ★ ★ ★ ★ "Thoroughly 'user-friendly' step-by-step guide... so valuable for men and women striving to form, nurture, instil and live the values they hold dear."

—JAMES A. COX, MIDWEST BOOK REVIEW

★ ★ ★ ★ ★ "A fresh approach to parenting in the modern world... I can't imagine anyone who wouldn't benefit from reading this book. Through his own experience, Gale helps your identify your own families 'core issues' without preaching to you, rather in a way that makes you feel as if you are having a conversation."

—ALAINE BUCKNALL, ROYAL REVIEW/QUEEN OF HAPPY ENDINGS

★ ★ ★ ★ ★ "This book offers realistic ways for families to build harmonious households. Unlike so many books on kids and families, this book is a great practical resource. I liked the fact that it provided specific examples to help you teach your children- and yourself- constructive relationship problem solving. *The book really delivers*!"

—D avid READER

★ ★ ★ ★ ★ "Scott Gale wrote a book every parent should read. It will make their lives easier, much more simple and fun."

—DONNA SOZIO, AUTHOR OF
NEVER TRUST A MAN IN ALLIGATOR LOAFERS

Your Family Constitution

A MODERN APPROACH TO FAMILY VALUES AND HOUSEHOLD STRUCTURE

A Step-by-Step Guide to:

- Reconnecting with your kids
- Anticipating and addressing issues
- Advancing family communication
- Enjoying parenting to the fullest

Scott Gale

Spectrum International Press
105 Symphony
Irvine, California, 92603, U.S.A.

978-0-9822961-3-4

Library of Congress Control Number: 2009901888

Cover and interior design by Bookcovers.com

The publisher gratefully acknowledges the many publishers and individuals who granted Spectrum International Press permission to reprint the cited material.

Greg Cravens: www.cravenscartoon.com

Michael Fry: www.unitedfeatures.com

ACKNOWLEDGEMENTS

I'd like to express my heartfelt gratitude to the people who made this book possible. Through this journey, I have had the opportunity to learn a lot about my friends, family and myself. I thank all who opened up to me and encouraged me to continue with the writing process.

I'd first like to thank my family: Karen, Jack and Max. Not only did they inspire me to create our Family Constitution in the first place, they enabled me to try different ideas in our home that I am able to share through this book. A special thanks to my wonderful wife, Karen, who financially supported the family through the difficult real estate slow down and ultimately afforded me the opportunity to produce this book. I love you very much and look forward to many years of continued improvement together.

To my parents, Jay and Fran, thank you for guiding me successfully into adulthood. I'm fortunate that you ingrained values, work ethic and personal drive in my soul. Now, as a parent, I appreciate the challenges you faced raising me and Erica. I am extremely grateful that you had the perseverance to keep us moving in the right direction...I now know it was no easy task.

Thank you to Donna Sozio for the wonderful advice. You truly helped me shape my message and organize my book for public consumption. Because of your efforts, I spent twice the time writing, but ended up with a book that is ten times better.

Sincere thanks to Lindsay Coluccio, Amy Ferry, Sara Waters, Julie Gotz, and Jo Strapp. I appreciate your feedback and edits, but more importantly, I thank you for sharing your stories with me and for making the effort to try my techniques.

Finally, thank you to my fantastic business partners: Mike Kerr, Ralph Emerson and Bentley Kerr. You have all stood patiently by me while I poured my effort into this book. One of these days there will be a real estate market again. I look forward to many prosperous years together once it arrives.

CONTENTS

Foreword by Jay Gale, Ph.D.

FAMILY THERAPIST • AUTHOR'S FATHER

As a practicing clinical psychologist who has dealt with dysfunctional family relationships for almost four decades, I've learned a lot about people and their families. I've heard the tales of busy parents trying to maintain sanity in a world changing at a frantic pace. I've seen the family unit change, with more than 50% of marriages now ending in divorce. And I've witnessed passionate displays of the full spectrum of parental emotions.

Having two children of my own, one of whom authored this book, I realize that you don't have to have a Ph.D. to appreciate how difficult, frustrating, magical and rewarding parenting can be. Parenting is the hardest job I have ever had. However, it is also the highlight of my life and the experience which I am most proud of. It is a gift and an honor to be a parent.

From my own personal experiences as a parent and from listening to the trials and tribulations of my patients, I have identified a few points that any parent with kids in the house should know:

> ➤ The world is different today from the way it was yesterday and the way it will be tomorrow.

> ➤ If you want to get the most out of parenthood, you must allow the unique pleasures of parenting to outshine the more aggravating aspects of the job. If you don't enjoy it the first time around, the opportunity is quickly gone.

> ➤ If you want to do the best job you can as a parent, make good use of the resources at your disposal.

Fundamental respect and discipline have been casualties at all levels of our culture. You see it in corporate greed, in governmental arrogance, and in the many athletes who forget that they are part of a team. So, it is no surprise that with so many poor role models constantly in the headlines, "youth entitlement," as many refer to it today, is a real concern.

Many parents overlook the gravity of this cultural shift, dismissing the obvious symptoms of entitlement as "kids just being kids." However, the *life-long* consequences of failing to impart accountability in a child, as well as constantly excusing his self-centered and apathetic behavior, can be devastating to his development and outlook.

The principles of human learning are clear. If a child (or an adult) commits an act and finds the results rewarding, he will tend to repeat that act. That's why unaddressed bad habits tend to grow and fester.

Realistically, you can't be on top of every potentially negative situation with your child. We live in a world of rapid change and cultural shifts that challenge even the most involved parents. But you can, and must, be instrumental in helping your child to develop a healthy mindset and promote positive values such as a strong work ethic, respect and a sense of appreciation. These simple principles can make an enormous difference in a child's ability to cope, and save him from pain and lost opportunities while adjusting to a world where people don't cater to his needs.

When my children were in their growing years, the resources were extremely limited by today's standards, both in quantity and quality. There was no WebMD.com to look up medical advice. There were no online support groups from which to glean guidance, and the books that were available were dry and outdated.

As a parent, I often fell back on the source of knowledge I was most familiar with: memories from my own childhood and the recollections of the things my parents had done (or not done) while raising me. I wish I'd had the benefit of today's parenting tools when my son and daughter were still in the house. A book like *Your Family Constitution* could have helped smooth out some bumpy family turbulence by opening up the lines of communication and allowing us the opportunity to clarify our family's boundaries.

I'm very proud of Scott for recognizing the need to bring change to his own family, taking the time to initiate his innovative ideas, and now sharing his experiences with other parents. As I read through *Your Family Constitution* I realized Scott has figured out the critical nature of self-understanding, spousal teamwork and effective communication, as well as how to integrate these ingredients into his family dynamic. More importantly to me, Scott has discovered a simple and effective way to establish boundaries for his children. My grandkids respect the rules because they helped create them. They know their voices were heard as their Family Constitution evolved.

Your Family Constitution doesn't provide absolute answers; no parenting tool does. Your family is unique. However, the process of establishing a Family Constitution will lead you on a special journey that will provide a process for finding your own solutions. Even if you never create your own Family Constitution, you cannot help but take away Scott's inspiring message... Don't settle for surviving as a parent. Make every minute count with your kids. Don't let frustration damage the most important and rewarding relationships that you will ever experience during your short time on this planet.

SECTION 1:
OUR FAMILY CONSTITUTION

Introduction

BLACK SUNDAY AND THE ROAD TO ROCK BOTTOM

"A family is a place where minds come in contact with one another. If these minds love one another, the home will be as beautiful as a flower garden. But if these minds get out of harmony with one another, it is like a storm that plays havoc with the garden."

—BUDDHA

BLACK SUNDAY

Mother's Day 2007, our celebration was in full-stride. My wife, two sons and I had just finished up a nice brunch with my parents and headed for the beach. The sun was shining. The sound of breaking waves soothed my soul as we walked on the sand. I felt good. These were the moments I had signed up for when I became a dad. Then my nine year-old son Jack started complaining.

It began with a whine about not going to the tide pools. Then he moaned about having to share a ball with his brother. Finally, he rolled his eyes in objection when I asked him not to go into the water past his knees to avoid getting his clothes wet. I could have overlooked or ignored any of these gripes independently, but the rapid succession with which they came, combined with the thick cloud of tension that already hung over us, had loosened my self-control. In an instant, I exploded.

I first reacted by hollering at him to stop his antics. All I got in return was more complaining. I quickly moved on to a series of idle threats in a desperate attempt to end the charade. Other people on the beach were looking at me, wondering why I was shouting "You're done with TV for a week!", "You're going to bed right after dinner!" and "You can spend the rest of the day in your bedroom!" I couldn't stop. My actions were guided by a very angry autopilot.

My intimidation tactics failed. Jack countered my tyrannical rant with the all-too-familiar "stink-eye" and crossed arms. As the scene escalated, my wife Karen became engaged, visibly upset with both Jack and me. She clearly wanted to put an end to the spectacle. At first she tried to make peace, but promptly moved on to angry protest herself when she realized there was no accord in sight.

By that time, my bridge to reason had collapsed under a flood of emotion. I resorted to name-calling and absurd proclamations such as "Listen here you selfish jerk, we are leaving...now!" and "If you want a ride home, you better shower off and

be ready to go by the time we are!" I mixed in a few expletives to punctuate my message. I was losing it.

Jack walked away, feigning refusal to leave with us. Karen stormed towards the car, clearly disgusted, in disbelief of what she had just witnessed. My younger son Max and I silently moved towards the showers to clean our feet. After washing off the sand, I took a brief moment to collect myself.

As Max and I walked to the car, I noticed Jack shadowing us from several paces behind, no doubt wanting to ensure we would not call his bluff and leave without him. He didn't say a word. He didn't have to. The hurt and anger on his face told the story.

Finally, we arrived at the car and all got in, including Jack. The tension at that moment was more intense than we had ever experienced together. Karen was frazzled, but decided to drive anyway. She pulled onto the main street and nearly collided with a passing vehicle. My blood pressure notched up to a record high. Once again, I lost it. I yelled at her and criticized her driving abilities.

What happened next is still subject to debate. Considering there was no video replay and no clear account, it's destined to be an unsolved mystery forever. Karen recalls that I asked her to pull over so I could get out of the car. I, however, remember leaving at her request. Regardless of the reason, she stopped the car and I got out. I closed the door and she drove off.

Perhaps I was delusional. Maybe I just underestimated the distance home or the blazing heat. Either way, I started the twelve-mile hike home up Laguna Canyon Road in my flip-flops. I had a cell phone and could have called for a ride. Or, I could have turned around and returned to the beach. Instead, I opted to punish myself with a really long walk.

Karen called me a short while later to see how I faired. The Sunday afternoon traffic towards Laguna Beach was now so horrendous that I couldn't ask her to return and pick me up. Besides, my foolish pride prohibited me from making such a bold request. She suggested a taxi, but I told her I was walking, perhaps vindictively trying to manufacture guilt for her driving off without me.

I walked and walked and walked, succeeding in my quest to punish myself. As if the walk hadn't been long enough, I encountered a park ranger who turned me back as I attempted to shortcut across a private trail towards my home. In the end, it took more than four hours to make the trek. It was worth every second.

THE DAWN OF REALITY

During my long journey home, I spent most of the time contemplating our family situation. Certain things rose to the surface and became clear. I realized that losing my patience with Jack was due to my inability to communicate effectively. I had been trying to shape his behavior through random directives and disciplinary actions. His habitual eye-rolls, verbal push-back and disrespect, which I'd interpreted as innate animosity towards me, had, in reality, been his coping mechanisms for dealing with my lack of clarity.

When I finally arrived home, it was clear we all hurt deeply from what had transpired. But on top of the hurt, there was anger. I felt at fault for the incident, but couldn't shake the resentment, nor could they. It took a day or so before we could begin to forgive and openly talk about the Mother's Day debacle. By that time, I'd already discovered we had underlying issues to settle if we wanted to ensure that we didn't repeat this kind of family meltdown.

I knew it deep inside my heart. Something *had* to change.

THE ROAD TO ROCK BOTTOM

In hindsight, I'm surprised that it took so long for the situation to come to a head. My family had few *clear* rules or *firm* behavioral standards. We had no *consistent* consequences and no *mutual* basis of understanding from which to discuss our challenges. These problems had been in front of me the whole time, but my eyes had been closed. My long walk home opened them to reality.

The volcano erupted on Black Sunday, but the pressure between me and Jack had been building for quite some time. We had experienced a series of abrasions leading up to that day that had never healed. Each new rift magnified and aggravated the raw emotional wounds.

The first sore spot developed on the baseball diamond. That season, I had volunteered to be an assistant coach. It started out fine, but as the season wore on, Jack routinely ignored my coaching advice and complained each time I addressed his behavior.

I felt embarrassed and frustrated by the fact that I couldn't get through to my own kid. I had no influence on his development as a player and no ability to stop him from fooling around. My continual attempts to call Jack out only made him resentful, as well as more obstinate and determined to act like a clown.

Next there was Rusty, the puppy we purchased for Jack's birthday in March, just three weeks before Black Sunday. I had promised Jack when he was five that he could get a dog when he turned nine, if and only if *he* made the commitment to take care of it. I fulfilled my end of the bargain, despite my concern about adding more chaos to our already frantic household.

At first, Jack took care of Rusty as agreed. But, as the sparkle faded, Jack's enthusiasm for taking care of a puppy waned. The work associated with owning a dog interfered with his other pursuits. He complained each time I reminded him of his commitment. My lectures about responsibility fell on deaf ears, evoking only defensiveness and anger.

Finally, Jack and his younger brother quarreled incessantly about which show to watch, whose turn it was to play video games, or who got more popcorn. I had no interest in mediating their squabbles and no intention of settling their petty issues.

When an argument between Jack and Max escalated to screaming or hitting, I would reluctantly get sucked in. I usually yelled or sent them to the room they shared. Unfortunately, my reaction typically spurred more fighting, as Jack and Max inevitably had to dispute who was at fault for getting me mad.

In the wake of Black Sunday, my family problems felt deep and complicated. The solutions seemed elusive. I felt the need to understand our situation. Full comprehension represented the only viable way to mend my wounded family. I wanted to feel like a real dad again, not the angry guy I had become. When I finally took the time to look within, the things I discovered surprised me.

I realized that for 10 years, my wife Karen and I had been continuously juggling three bowling balls: our kids, our personal needs and our careers. It had been exhausting, painful and awkward at times, but too much had been at stake to let any of the balls hit the ground.

The balls grew heavier each year. The kids joined more teams and had more practices. Karen and I each took on more responsibility at work. Birthday parties abounded every weekend. In short, our world got crazier by the moment.

Our sheer determination had enabled us to keep the balls from crashing for a decade, but resolve alone could no longer ensure perseverance. Incremental stresses had slowly mounted to the point where an outward venting of emotion, like Black Sunday, seemed like the only way to purge frustration.

Our love for each other had kept my family intact, but daily pressures had severely eroded our mutual respect and understanding. We urgently needed to change course to avoid irreparable damage. My family had traveled to Rock Bottom with me in the driver's seat. I had no choice but to make a u-turn and try to find the road out.

Rock Bottom was a state of mind for me. I struggled to find satisfaction during my day-to-day interactions with my kids. My pessimism overshadowed my family's many blessings. My negative emotional responses aggravated existing tensions. I dragged the people I loved most down with me. Fear, frustration and anxiety became the staples of family life.

The truth is that I didn't even know we were headed towards Rock Bottom until we had arrived. Throughout this book, I'll share with you the signs and symptoms I recognized in hindsight. If you think you might be on the hidden highway to your own Rock Bottom, hopefully my experiences can help your family reverse course before you get there.

The Nature of Our Dysfunction

There were multiple layers to the dysfunction which landed my family at Rock Bottom. On the surface there were the abrasive situations (e.g. baseball, Rusty, arguing) that routinely provoked conflict. These *visible* irritants received the blame for our problems, but they were not the root causes.

Beneath the surface lurked my family's *core* issues, ingrained problems that were both hard to identify and painful to accept. I had to understand these deep-rooted challenges if I were to have any hope of addressing our troubles. I needed to examine my family's darkest layers of dysfunction.

Core Issue #1: Lack of Time

What do you get when you cross two working professionals, two active kids and a dog? Chaos! To get off Rock Bottom, I knew I needed to create more time for my kids, my marriage and myself. I desperately wanted to keep up with the necessities of daily life, but could only afford to focus on the hottest fires. As the years went by and the kids got more involved in activities, the fabric of our family gradually stretched thinner and thinner until it started to tear.

The stress of our constant struggle to keep up took its toll. Communication between Karen and I grew evermore difficult. We were drowning in our own schedules. By Black Sunday, Karen and I were simply too stymied and fatigued to keep the balls in the air any longer.

Core Issue #2: Lack of Clarity

My parental expectations had never been clear, not even to myself. In the absence of clarity, I resorted to "thematic parenting." I used haphazard mandates to encourage nondescript guidelines. I gave Jack and Max varying instructions to reinforce recurrent behavioral "themes." I suppose I figured my kids could read between my thematic lines and interpret my underlying messages. I was wrong. Confusion ensued.

For instance, I often attempted to get Jack and Max to play outside. My intentions were good. I wanted to encourage my kids to be active. Most Saturdays, I would tell Jack and Max to turn the TV off after breakfast. Sometimes, I would deliver the message after lunch. On weekends when I was worn down or focused on something else, I might let them watch all day.

Jack and Max couldn't possibly manage their weekend schedules around my whims. My ever-changing mandates never established concrete expectations of when or how much television they could watch. A positive and reliable routine might have helped my boys develop

healthy habits. Erratic themed instructions never had a chance.

The kids grew frustrated. They used my mixed messages against me. They argued precedents such as "You let us watch all day last Saturday" to justify more television. I was frustrated by my lack of clarity too. Unfortunately, that was the price I had to pay for substituting "themes" for a clear set of rules.

Core Issue #3: Lack of Consistency

Even for the few rules that were clear (i.e. homework before television), Karen and I had no uniform method to enforce them. We simply did not have the physical, mental or emotional capacity to consistently uphold discipline in the midst of our hectic lives. Our reaction to any given circumstance depended on our current mood, energy level and mental fortitude.

For example, Jack and Max knew they could postpone their bedtime each night by testing mine and Karen's parental resolve. They would usually open up with a sheepish request to "stay up five minutes longer" or to "finish the show." When feeling more determined, they might declare injustice or recite the many reasons why we should allow them to stay up. Regardless of their approach, Jack and Max failed to hit the sack, as requested.

Karen and I had a nightly choice to make: concession or combat. Neither option felt right. It boiled down to a question of resolve. Sometimes Karen would take one approach and I would take the other. I felt like we couldn't win. At the time, we were painfully unaware of our third option— structure.

Core Issue #4:

Lack of Commitment to Improvement

With so many "important" things to get done, my family focused on near-term survival. We never stepped back to reflect. We never tried to evaluate or understand how we functioned as a team. We didn't recognize the positive impacts such an effort might have.

The kids got older. We all got busier. The problems grew more complicated. The luster of our interrelationships began to fade. We *needed* a force to intervene, but we were painfully oblivious to this fact.

Looking back, my family expended far too much time and effort on battle. We could have re-channeled our energy. We could have taken our eyes off of the "bowling balls" for a moment and focused our efforts on improving our long-term family dynamic.

Unfortunately, my family was caught in a rut. We had become accustomed to confrontation and emotional bruising. Our frenzied pace veiled the urgent need for change. It took the Black Sunday meltdown to enlighten me. Better late than never.

RAY OF HOPE

I have always subscribed to the old adage "Luck is what happens when preparation meets opportunity." The aftermath of Black Sunday mentally and emotionally prepared me to address my family's problems. Under unexpected circumstances, I found the right opportunity to unite with my preparation.

I created my own luck and pieced together a tool capable of picking my family up and putting us back together. I called it the "Family Constitution." Over time, it became the catalyst for clarity, consistency and commitment in my family. These "3-C's" became the glue that re-attached us. The Family Constitution would finally enable my family to have the critical structure that we'd lacked for so long.

I knew the journey from Rock Bottom would be demanding, even with our Family Constitution to smooth out the bumps. But for the first time in a while, I held onto sincere hope.

My vision eventually proved to have substance beyond my initial expectations. My family realized immediate forward progress and we have continued to improve steadily ever since. The issues weren't nearly as complicated as I had originally thought.

The key was taking the time to examine my family's problems. I investigated our issues from the roots up, first trying to understand myself and my family at a very basic level, then looking at the challenges that plagued us. Once I had diagnosed our ailments and remedied them with structure, the healing commenced and the emotional barriers began to come down.

WHAT'S AHEAD?

In the chapters that follow, I'll share the details of our Family Constitution and explain why it worked for us. More importantly, I'll reveal the *step-by-step process* I went through to get my family back on track.

My family's set of problems and solutions is unique to us. The exercise of simply reading our rules may spark a few ideas, perhaps even provide solutions to a few common issues. However, as was the case for me during my search for "quick fix" answers, hasty attempts to apply someone else's structure to your own family will inevitably prove to be fruitless.

I will guide you through the process of creating your own Family Constitution. During the journey, I'll share many personal stories of my successes and failures as a parent. Some are funny, some sad and others just plain weird. Nonetheless, each represents a lesson learned, from which I grew as a dad and a person.

I hope my experiences convince you of the fact that you are not alone in your parental challenges. More importantly, I hope that you can utilize the lessons from my trials and tribulations to make your own family stronger.

Chapter 1

MY JOURNEY BEGINS

"I have always looked at life as a voyage, mostly wonderful, sometimes frightening. In my family and friends I have discovered treasure more valuable than gold."

—JIMMY BUFFET

A fter the Black Sunday blow-up, I didn't know what to do or where to go to for help. I just knew my family needed change. I started at the bookstore, feverishly looking through the parenting section, trying to find that golden piece of advice that would solve all of my problems.

I read several books and flipped through a few others. Many referenced "entitlement", the moniker of a modern youth culture convinced of their divine right to self-indulgence, ease and entertainment. I recognized this attitude in my own children. Truth be told, I even identified some shades of entitlement in myself; leading me to believe the entitlement movement may have started slowly rolling decades ago.

I read and read, trying to absorb the observations and advice of the many experts whose books I had purchased. The books seemed to fall into one of two categories: those written to educate and those written to entertain. Unfortunately, both genres narrowly missed my target. In order to start the healing process, I needed a blend of sound parenting philosophy and practical application. I couldn't find that combination anywhere.

The educational books disbursed sensible theory, but they didn't communicate how to *apply* their theories to my family situation. They completely skipped over the vital importance of introspection and observation during the problem-solving process.

The entertainment books produced laughs and legitimately made me feel less isolated. The trying experiences of other parents helped me put my problems into perspective and inadvertently forced me to dig into my psyche. The challenge these books inevitably faced was that the how-to message got lost in translation. I needed practicality. Loosely coordinated anecdotes just didn't deliver.

In hindsight, fundamental lack of self-understanding had impeded my ability to relate advice to my own circumstances. I had looked fervently for an immediate solution, unaware of my failure to lay introspective groundwork.

The quick-fix solution that I sought was the adult equivalent of Santa Claus— fascinating and fantastic, but not grounded in reality. I held onto the hope that immediate answers existed for as long as I could. But eventually reality set in. No magic potions, pills, chants or books could fix my family's problems overnight. The escape from Rock Bottom was destined to be a sustained journey.

FAMILY AND FANTASY FOOTBALL

Inspiration comes from the craziest places. On a rare, lazy Saturday a couple of months after Black Sunday, a silent bell went off in my head. I was sprawled out on a lawn chair, deep in thought, diligently preparing for my Fantasy Football draft.

The Not Quite Executive Fantasy Football League (NQEFFL) verged on its second season. The formal adoption of our league rules would be the primary topic of discussion at our upcoming meeting of "franchise owners."

Our league format was unprecedented. As such, no template rules had existed to assist us in shaping our league structure. During our first franchise owners' meeting in June 2006, we had recognized the experimental nature of our inaugural season. Accordingly, we had agreed to reconvene during the summer of 2007 to reflect and adjust accordingly before formalizing the rules.

In preparation for the impending meeting, our league commissioner had clearly defined every nuance of proposed league policy in the NQEFFL Constitution— a 15-page document which he had distributed to all franchise owners for review. It covered every operational aspect of our league, including technical rules, dispute resolution procedures, an amendment process and even an owner conduct policy.

The NQEFFL Constitution represented the perfect by-product of effort, organization and creativity. It infused structure and communication into Fantasy Football, a space where beer and chaos had traditionally reigned. The NQEFFL Constitution effectively removed confusion and emotion from the decision-making process, allowing franchise owners to build *our* Fantasy Football league to best represent *our* collective needs.

As I sat on my lawn chair, reviewing the NQEFFL Constitution, my mind wandered towards Jack. Then, in an instant, it happened. Fantasy Football, parental theory and Jack melded in my mind. I realized I could thoughtfully apply the constitutional framework to address my family's need for clarity, consistency and commitment. I reclined for a moment to contemplate the possibilities. The Family Constitution had been conceived!

FIRST STEPS

Following my epiphany, I promptly whittled down the frame of the NQEFFL Constitution, converting its purpose from Fantasy Football to family reality. With a functional template in hand, I turned to Karen, Jack and Max for input. I wanted them to be part of the process. I hoped they would provide topics and ideas that I could incorporate into our Family Constitution.

They unanimously declined my invitation to participate. I sensed their collective doubt, but I would not be deterred. I spent the summer putting together a draft Family Constitution using the only input I could get— my own. I laid out a tiered process to understand my family's needs and build structure around them. It started with a look inside myself and ultimately finished with concrete boundaries and incentives. Each sequential step in between expanded on the findings of the one that preceded it.

Following a couple of months of observation, focused effort and repeated trial and error, I finalized my first complete draft. Karen, Jack, Max and I sat down together to talk through our new structure, fill in a few blanks (i.e. appropriate bedtimes) and make necessary adjustments before it took effect. Then, four months after Black Sunday, we formally adopted our inaugural Family Constitution.

We all had to adjust and compromise to make it work, but eventually we each found elements that we appreciated and could relate to. Our Family Constitution still had a long way to go before I could declare the experiment a complete success. Nonetheless, my family's dynamics genuinely improved.

WALK BEFORE YOU RUN

Throughout the remainder of this book, I'll refer to our inaugural Family Constitution as the "First Attempt". Like the initial NQEFFL rules, the First Attempt represented a starting point for my family, not a destination. In reality, it took several months just to upgrade my family's response to the Family Constitution from "tolerate" to "accept."

During the First Attempt, my family made tangible progress. Our communication skills improved tremendously. Our penchant for heated debates subsided. And, we learned a lot about ourselves and each other.

Despite these improvements, Karen, Jack and Max never fully embraced my ideas and never provided me with their own. To reach its full potential, our Family Constitution required vital changes. First and foremost, I had to generate real enthusiasm. I needed Karen and the boys to understand that, with their full support and contribution, the Family Constitution could improve our lives and interrelationships far beyond where we currently stood.

Nine months into the First Attempt, I made a choice to pull the plug. Recognizing the need for substantial restructuring, I vacillated between amending the First Attempt and starting from scratch. I decided a fresh start gave our Family Constitution the best chance to move past awkward baby steps.

In preparation for a second attempt ("Take Two"), I let the First Attempt die. It had served its purpose, but the time had come to let go of its structure and clean the slate. When I stopped enforcing the rules, my family followed suit. Our household gradually slipped back into old patterns.

REACHING OUT

Despite its initial shortcomings, I took great pride in our Family Constitution. For months after its inception, it was my new baby. Like any proud father, I wanted to pass out a few cigars and introduce it to the important people in my life. Through casual conversation, I began to share my concept with friends and family, describing some of our rules and the impacts they had made.

As I let people into my family's inner sanctum, many invited me into theirs. Some offered up tales from their childhood, others described challenges they faced as parents. The stories I got differed as much as the people who told them; yet they delivered a universal message. Every family had encountered highs and lows. Everyone had experienced their own Black Sunday. I wasn't a bad parent, I was just a parent.

Many people requested a copy of our Family Constitution. Slowly but surely, feedback trickled in. No one used our Family Constitution verbatim, but many extracted ideas. They modified elements of our structure to suit their own family's needs. They introduced chores to their kids, eliminated routine arguments in their homes, and held family meetings to improve their communication.

Our Family Constitution made a difference! It got my family off Rock Bottom. It made me a better parent. Now, it improved my friends' families as well. Thank goodness Black Sunday opened my eyes. Thank goodness for fantasy football.

Chapter 2

WHAT THE HECK IS A FAMILY CONSTITUTION?

"There are no problems we cannot solve together, and very few that we can solve by ourselves."

—LYNDON B. JOHNSON

THE UNITED STATES CONSTITUTION

(Philadelphia, Pennsylvania, 1787)

"We the People of the United States, in Order to form a more perfect Union, establish Justice, insure domestic Tranquility, provide for the common defence, promote the general Welfare, and secure the Blessings of Liberty to ourselves and our Posterity, do ordain and establish this Constitution for the United States of America."

These famous words represent the guiding principles of the original United States Constitution, as well the 27 amendments that would eventually follow. Fifty-five Founding Fathers produced this historic text during the summer of 1787, as they established a vision for a new nation.

Through months of careful thought, heated debate and unprecedented compromise, these Founding Fathers balanced the interest of 13 sovereign states to create the document that would be the platform of freedom for centuries to come. They may not have appreciated the full magnitude of their achievement; nevertheless, what they accomplished *together* was nothing short of remarkable.

THE FAMILY CONSTITUTION

(Irvine, California, 2007)

The U.S. Constitution set the basis for a new nation. The NQEFFL Constitution established unity amongst 12 fantasy football franchise owners. The Family Constitution instituted a firm household foundation for four individuals and a dog.

The scale and application of each of these constitutions vary tremendously. However, the documents bear certain resemblances. The same basic principles (unity, justice, tranquility and promotion of common welfare) guide purpose and process. Each document permanently changed the human dynamic between its constituents. Finally, each constitution established a platform for effective growth, capable of evolving over time.

So, what is a Family Constitution? How did it enable my family to progress? Keep reading. I'm about to explain the driving forces behind our Family Constitution. I'm about to share the most important lessons that I ever learned as a dad.

Rewards and Consequences

Our Family Constitution relies on compounding rewards and consequences to steer behavior. Jack and Max's positive choices result in allowance, sleepovers and other privileges. Rewards increase with continuity, motivating the kids to maintain a streak of good performance.

Likewise, poor decisions by Jack and Max compel escalating consequences. Extra chores get layered on. They lose privileges such as television and the right to visit friends. They go to bed early. They spend time alone in their room. They do push-ups, sit-ups and laps around our block.

Our Family Constitution demands performance by Mom and Dad too, but with different targets and incentives. Karen and I have our own assigned chores. We're prohibited from yelling, whining and name-calling, just like the kids. I workout three times each week to earn the right to watch football on Sundays.

Although the real reward for us is a functional family, Karen and I can also earn the right to select family outings, games and meals. Our consequences for inappropriate behavior are identical to the kids'. I've done sit-ups and push-ups when I've raised my voice. I've contributed money to a swear jar after letting bad words slip. By accepting these consequences, I'm able to demonstrate the importance of abiding by our Family Constitution.

The common thread between my family members and me is that we are all responsible for our own actions. We all face consequences of appropriate magnitude which guide our decisions. We all hold each other accountable for following the household rules that we agreed upon in our Family Constitution.

Understanding and Empowerment

Our Family Constitution embodies mutual understanding and empowerment. We leverage honest communication and joint focus to produce an agreed upon set of household standards. The rules are the rules. No need for argument or debate.

We empower our Family Constitution to create the behavioral choices for us. Karen, Jack, Max and I each recognize the finite impacts of our actions. Carefully selected boundaries, combined with absolute rewards and consequences, effectively guide behavior. Good decisions improve the quality of our individual and collective lives. All things considered, the right choice usually qualifies as the most desirable option.

Simplicity

Adjusting to new rules and routines takes both energy and resolve. I desperately wanted my family to succeed without frustration and resentment. For that reason, our Family Constitution started simple.

We started small and allowed our structure to grow. We chose to address only a few immediate issues at first, including bedtime, chores and television usage. We surrounded these basic issues with straightforward boundaries and rules. We set the stage for immediate success.

WHERE'S THE PAYOFF?

The Family Constitution is a sustained investment in family. It takes time, energy and commitment. So where is the payoff? How long does it take to reap the benefits?

The short answer is that the process of creating a Family Constitution is an investment in faith. The timing and amount of return on invested effort depends entirely on the particular family's focus, personalities and circumstances.

Remember, my family's problems didn't clear up overnight. Some issues still have yet to be addressed. But, the simple fact is that we made progress. We got better in each of the ways that I'll describe below. I'm very proud of that accomplishment.

Time and Efficiency

Our Family Constitution put precious time back in our lives. As we built structure, we examined our family dynamic and became more efficient. We redistributed household responsibilities, changed our method of recording and keeping appointments, and reshuffled our scheduled activities.

We also reduced time spent on debate. Firm structure meant fewer issues to clash over. Many time-consuming and emotionally-taxing arguments faded in the wake of clarity and consistency. Not only do we now find ourselves with more time, the quality of our time together has dramatically improved.

Communication

The Family Constitution process broke down barriers to communication. As my family went through the steps, we talked through issues and found solutions together. We gained understanding of each others' concerns. We replaced fear and indifference in our interpersonal relationships with respect, appreciation and trust.

At our weekly family meetings, we now plan and coordinate schedules and needs for coming weeks. We discuss current issues and anticipate concerns on the horizon. We put everything out on the table to ensure we don't again reach the point of meltdown.

Accountability

Our Family Constitution established individual accountability, assigning distinct responsibilities and expectations to each family member. If a chore isn't done, we know who slipped. If Jack or Max misses his bedtime, he can no longer blame it on extraneous circumstances.

I had desired to teach responsibility to my kids for a long time. Unfortunately, I never knew how or when to do it. Our Family Constitution has proven to be the perfect instructional forum, as each of us has a distinct role and we can effectively review performance at our weekly family meeting.

Values

The Family Constitution enabled Karen and me to better impart our standards and beliefs upon our kids. The constitutional process caused both of us to examine ourselves and define our core family values. We talked openly and wove our independent ideals into an integrated vision. We built structure around our shared principles.

Improved communication also enabled Karen and me to talk to Jack and Max about sensitive issues without emotional discharge. We now serve as better role models because we're more relaxed. As a family, we anticipate and discuss upcoming matters each year, as we prepare for our annual amendment. In this way, Karen and I can express our beliefs and parental concerns to our boys before they must make critical choices.

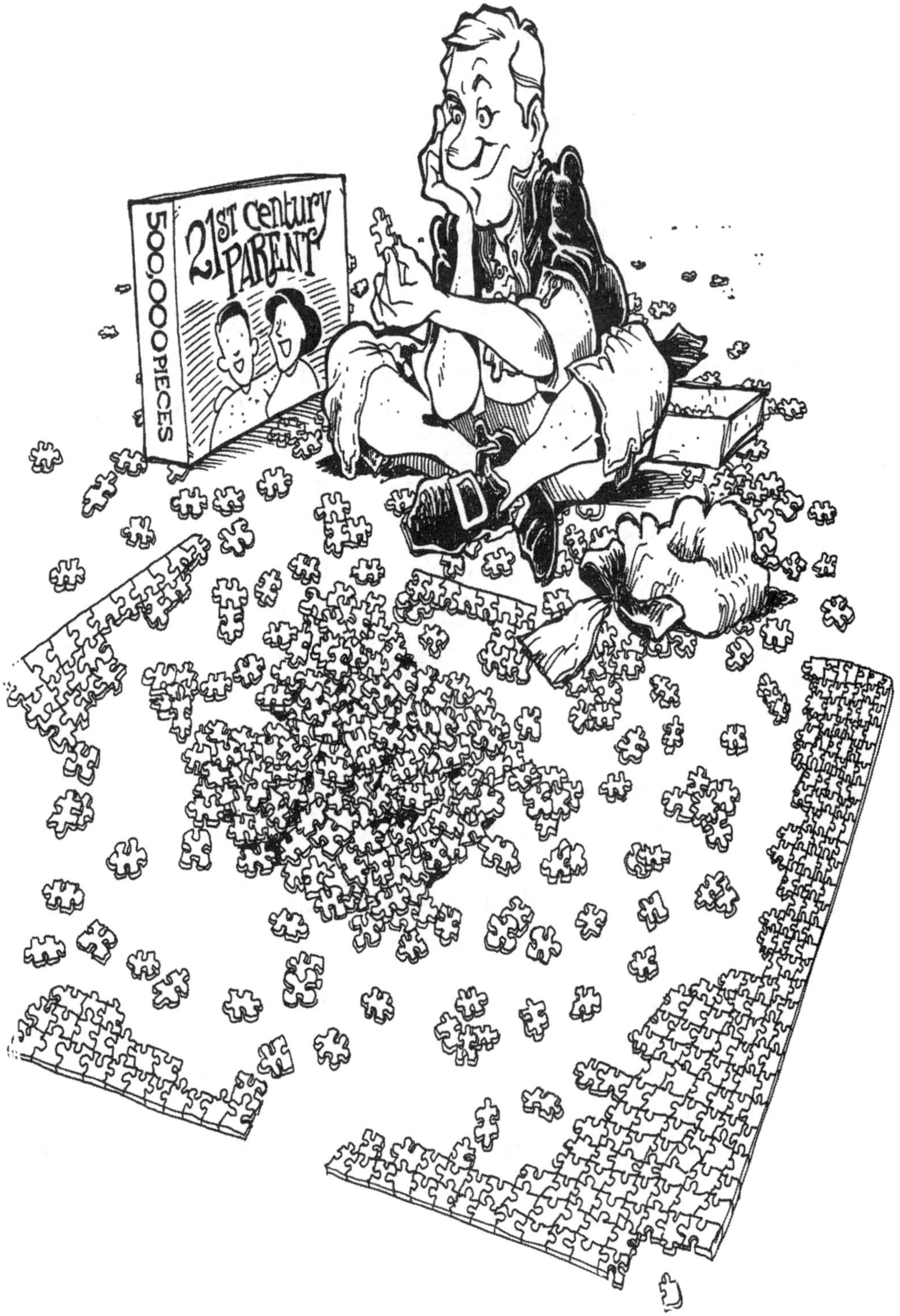
21ST Century PARENT
500,000 PIECES

Chapter 3

THAT WAS THEN. THIS IS NOW....
THE ANXIETIES OF MODERN PARENTS

"This is a time of soaring expectations and crushing realities."

—JEAN TWENGE

THE AGE OF AQUARIUS

I was born in 1970, the oldest of two children by liberal baby boomers. They had gone through the Cultural Revolution. Their generation had changed the world. Consciously or unconsciously, they bred their new-found sense of freedom in me.

For a few blissful years, the universe actually revolved around me. As such, I grew to expect comfort and convenience. My mom would take the phone off the hook when I slept to prevent its noisy ring from awakening my precious soul. For a good long while, I represented their pride and joy. During that period, they wouldn't dare stop the earth from orbiting around my needs.

Unfortunately, I eventually lost my coveted spot at the center of the universe. I began to interact with other kids whose parents had also instilled a sense of great self-importance in them. Slowly but surely, we mutually chipped away at each others' self-delusions.

Somewhere along the way, my parents also changed their tune. My mom and dad each grew up during the post-WWII era when behavioral standards and discipline were considered "part of life." Looking back, it was inevitable that those ideals would surface in their parenting efforts; nevertheless, I grimaced each time miserable terms such as "earn your keep," "elbow grease," and "just do it" echoed through our home.

Eventually, I did myself what many generations of kids had done before me. I sucked it up. I adjusted my expectations. Chores, work and responsibility became part of life. I may not have liked it, but I quickly got the message.

As time passed, something unexpected and a little disconcerting happened. I began to like work. I liked the money and kudos I received for doing chores and odd jobs. I felt good about being able to contribute to my family's well-being. Most importantly, I learned to appreciate my free time more, as I had less of it.

I don't know if it was part of my parents' "grand plan," but three decades ago, their fortitude ingrained motivation and self-discipline deep in my soul. As an adult, I have never looked back with regret. I feel truly blessed my parents didn't allow me to slide each time I made a fuss. I'm glad the universe stopped revolving around me when it did.

THE AGE OF ENTITLEMENT

Fast forward three decades. The world has changed dramatically. So has parenting. Life is faster. "What's in it for me?" has replaced "How can I help?" as the prevailing mentality. Lawsuits, information overload and cultural changes have degraded personal discipline and accountability in the classroom, work place and home. Deep-rooted appreciation, work ethic and values have become more the exception than the norm. Parents struggle to raise responsible and respectful kids. The Age of Entitlement is clearly upon us.

I first noticed it when Jack was about five. He embraced independence, insisting on choosing his own clothes and dressing himself. He had very resolute opinions for his age. He seemed ready to take on responsibility, so we pulled a play from my parents' playbook. We assigned basic chores and attempted to reign in his sense of deservedness. It didn't take.

Jack routinely forgot to do his chores. Each time, Karen and I barraged him with "reminders" until he eventually met his obligations. As time passed, we saved frustration by doing Jack's jobs for him. It seemed easier than bugging him. Something felt wrong.

We temporarily gave up. I attributed our failed experiment to Jack's young age. We tried again a year later, but again encountered a false start. He continued to "forget" to do his chores. He whined each time we prodded him. He expected us to do everything for him. Accountability simply didn't exist in Jack's vocabulary.

I once asked him to hang up his shirt. He asked "Why me?" So, I stated the obvious— "Because it's your shirt, Jack." He responded with the words "Yeah, it's mine, but you're the dad." There could be no more denial. Jack's resistance to work had developed into blatant entitlement.

After many incidents of the sort, I grew increasingly frustrated. I began to compare notes with my friends. I observed their techniques and family interactions.

I even watched kids on my baseball team communicate with their parents, hoping to glean ideas. I searched for clues. I wanted to know if I was alone. I wanted to find a cure for the malady that had infected my home.

As I watched, talked and listened to parents, it became obvious. I was not alone. Entitlement had become epidemic. I was witnessing a social movement. An entire generation of kids was growing up with a sense of privilege.

Entitlement in Action *("I Deserve Better... Don't I?")*

Bill wanted to get an SUV. He wanted to have some fun with the vehicle for a couple of years, then to pass it on to Ted, his 14 year-old son who planned to get his driver's license in two years. Bill made a deal with his son. If Ted washed the car regularly, inside and out, he could *have* it after he got his license. All he had to do was bathe the car a couple of times a month. The car would be Ted's to enjoy— no strings attached.

Upon making the deal, Bill spent approximately $25,000 buying the vehicle. At the time when I talked with Bill, he had owned the SUV for a year and had received exactly one car wash. When asked to fulfill his part of the bargain, Ted repeatedly claimed that he no longer liked the car and had no interest in driving it when he got his license.

Ted's cavalier attitude and sense of privilege exemplifies the "me first" approach to life which is so pervasive in today's youth culture. Entitlement is contagious. I'll do everything I can to keep Jack and Max from catching that infection.

MAKING SENSE OF MODERN ISSUES

I'm terrified. My success as a Dad hinges on my ability to navigate Jack and Max through obstacles that I frankly don't understand. I know cyberspace presents inherent dangers for young impressionable minds, but I don't know what the greatest threats are or how to stop them.

I've never been to a chat room. "LOL" represents my entire text message vocabulary. I don't know how to surf MySpace. Even if I could understand today's technological concerns, a new wave of issues will invariably emerge tomorrow.

Technology is just the tip of the iceberg. Kids today encounter powerful drugs at young ages. Violence is strewn across all forms of media. Unsafe sex can cost a young person his or her life. I want to equip Jack and Max to contend with these issues— but how?

A year before Black Sunday, I tried to figure it out. I scribbled three questions on a sheet of yellow paper during a moment of parental anxiety. I didn't have the answers. I didn't even know if they existed. However, at that moment, my success as a father depended on my ability to articulate the answers. I wrote:

1. How can I relate with the complex issues facing my kids?
2. How can I protect my kids from those issues that I simply can't understand?
3. How can I balance my desire to raise good kids with their desire to be independent?

I tried to think through the puzzle, but couldn't solve it. Eventually, my wave of anxiety passed. I gave up conscious effort to find answers. Nonetheless, I kept the questions in my private drawer. I glanced at the sheet of paper every month when I paid bills. Each time I placed it back in its spot, questions still unanswered.

Bridging the Generation Gap

One evening as I watched Jack play Madden NFL 08 on X-box 360, the first answer dawned on me through an epiphany of sorts. When I was his age, I loved playing video football with my friends on Intellivision, the finest gaming system of its time. Compared to its early-1980's competition, Intellivision boasted unrivaled graphics, controllers and game dynamics.

Intellivision's NFL Football was not nearly as fast, realistic or engaging as its modern counterpart, Madden NFL 08. Despite this, it inspired my competitive juices and incited rivalry with my friends just the same. As I watched Jack enjoy his game, I realized the relationship between Intellivision's NFL Football and Madden NFL 08 was a metaphor for life.

Life is not about the latest technology. It's about raw emotions and experiences. Kids today embrace the same things I did— competition, excitement, fun and companionship. They face the same fundamental issues too—expression, peer pressure, insecurities and schoolyard relationships. I could relate with these things; after all, I had lived through them. I could connect with my kids through my own experiences, just as I had with Madden NFL 2008.

To test my theory, I talked to my dad. He told me about his favorite childhood football game. He and his friends would strategically place plastic football players on a synthetic board shaped like a football field. To start the play, he would flip a switch. The board would vibrate and the plastic players would slowly move.

I asked about his emotional response to his electronic football game. He described to a tee the way I had felt playing Intellivision as a kid. "Competition, strategy, intensity and fun" were the operative words he used. Through three generations, the football games had grown exponentially faster, more complicated and visually appealing; however, the excitement level each produced hadn't changed a bit. That's irony.

Depending on the vantage point, technological advancements can be considered complications, conveniences or both. In absolute form, they are generational lifestyle differences, nuances produced by a continuous stream of innovation and circumstantial changes. Technology hasn't changed me as a person or a parent. The biggest difference between successive generations in my family is the quality of the tools and goodies we have access to.

Solving the Puzzle

I had now bridged the formidable generational gap that separated me from my children. I could finally throw away the yellow sheet of paper that contained my profound questions. Then the music stopped. I came back to reality. I had only answered question #1. Two important questions remained. In order to answer them, I had to return to my childhood.

I stepped out of the time machine in 1981, Queen's "Another One Bites the Dust" was penetrating the airwaves and the words "I want my MTV" were being spoken for the first time. I reminisced about my experiences and perspectives as a child. What moved me? What pushed me away?

Then I changed hats. I examined my childhood through the eyes of my dad. How had he understood my issues when I was a boy? How had he broken through our generational gap? How had he guided my choices without stifling my independence?

In an instant, I realized the *principles* of parenting hadn't really changed. In fact, the answers I had sought for so long mirrored the basic formula my parents had laid out while raising me and my sister.

Here are *the answers* I found:

☞ Parent to the *best of your abilities.*

☞ Make *good decisions* with the facts available. *Don't hesitate.*

☞ *Anticipate issues.* Address them before they become problems.

☞ Equip your kids to make good decisions. *Instill values, truth, confidence and responsibility.*

☞ *Don't be afraid to try and fail.* Learn from mistakes. *Improve with each day.*

☞ *Communicate* clearly. *Listen* intently. Keep an open mind. *Ask* a lot of questions.

☞ Use your *resources* wisely. *

☞ *Love* your kids *always.*

* Our Family Constitution later proved to be a huge resource; however, at the time I was focused on the value of mentors, support groups, books and other sources of advice.

I jotted down my thoughts and finally put away the yellow piece of paper for good. The "big questions" would menace me no longer.

PARENTING STYLES

I've found that there are three basic approaches to parenting: the *Easy Way,* the *Hard Way* and the *Constitutional Way.* Each requires varying amounts of effort. Each generates very different results. Most of us use some combination of all of these styles. We flip-flop back and forth depending on current circumstances and the emotional fortitude of ourselves and our children. We each have a style we rely on most. However, as was the case for me, we don't necessarily lean on the method we most prefer.

The Easy Way

The *Easy Way* is simple. It involves a steady diet of concessions, as well as a permanent blind-eye to misbehavior. This method facilitates temporary peace. However, routine spoiling inevitably breeds unsustainably high hopes in a child, resulting in disappointment, frustration, aggravation and despair for all.

The longer a parent travels down this path, the more difficult and painful it becomes to break from. The *Easy Way* often culminates with a public spectacle. Parents become humiliated while an uncomfortable silence falls over all others present.

WET BATHING SUIT BLUES

I once ended up at the beach unexpectedly with my friend Tom, his son Jerry, and my two boys. Even though the water was cold, the kids really wanted to go in the ocean. We had no bathing suits; so they swam in their shorts.

FRIENDS DON'T LET FRIENDS RAISE FRIENDS.

Friendship

YES, I KNOW. I UNDERSTAND WHY YOU'D WANT TO EAT CAKE FROSTING FOR BREAKFAST. IT'S YUMMY. IT'S CREAMY. AND IT HAS SPRINKLES... OH, WHAT THE HECK! JUST THIS ONCE...

Parenting

NO.

When they got out of the water, we had no spare clothes for them to change into. Jerry (eight) threw a tantrum because he didn't want to stay in wet shorts. Jack and Max would also have preferred fresh clothes, but they knew from experience that Jerry's approach wouldn't improve their situation. As Jerry cried, Jack and I shared a silent glance and smile to acknowledge my appreciation of Jack's patience.

Embarrassed, frustrated and wanting to avoid a scene, Tom handled the situation the *Easy Way*. He went to a nearby shop and bought Jerry a new pair of shorts. Upon his return, the uneasiness surrounding Jerry's outburst immediately lifted and we carried on with our fun activities.

Tom had successfully quashed a potential problem before it erupted, but Jerry had prevailed in the test of wills. Tom's actions reinforced Jerry's belief that melting down could get him what he wants. This familiar routine is destined to repeat itself again and again until Tom finally abandons the *Easy Way*.

The Hard Way

The *Hard Way* could be the most difficult and damaging method of parenting. It involves a mix of mental combat, idle threats and unchecked emotions. Unfortunately, I subscribed to this frustrating approach for several years.

The more I leaned on the *Hard Way*, the farther I pushed my family away. The lessons that I had fought so hard to teach my children couldn't penetrate their emotional barriers. The *Hard Way* paved my road to Rock Bottom.

FAMILY POKER

Family Poker is an integral part of the *Hard Way*. A game typically starts when parent or child throws down an ultimatum during confrontation. A series of bluffs and counter bluffs ensue. The stakes grow in force and effect with each successive bet. Eventually, the person with the losing hand concedes or blows up.

When kids are young, the game is simple and the deck almost always favors the parents. However, as kids get older and more sophisticated, Family Poker becomes more complicated and difficult. The stakes increase. Feelings get hurt. Credibility and self-esteem are put on the line. No one wins. There are just different degrees of losing.

Karen's friend Carol used the "all-in" bluff while trying to correct a problem with her teenage son, Mike. She told him if he couldn't follow the rules, then he wouldn't be welcome in her house. Carol didn't have winning cards and she couldn't afford to lose. Nonetheless, she pushed her chips out.

Unfortunately, Family Poker doesn't allow anyone to retract their bet. Her desperate attempt resulted in Mike's departure. He went to live with friends and didn't return. The *Hard Way* claimed another casualty on an ill-conceived bluff.

The Constitutional Way

During my first decade as a parent, I leaned heavily on both the *Easy Way* and *Hard Way* parenting methods. These were coping mechanisms. They allowed me to survive in situations when I didn't know what else to do. I couldn't find alternative parenting means. I didn't know where to start.

Since Black Sunday, I've learned to parent through structure, the *Constitutional Way*. This preferred method steers behavioral choices by leveraging mutual understanding, clear expectations and prescribed incentives. The *Constitutional Way* harnesses kids' energy and ideas, rather than dismissing their opinions.

Benjamin Franklin once said "An ounce of prevention is worth a pound of cure."

The *Constitutional Way* embodies this outlook. Weekly family meetings encourage open and honest communication between members of my fam-

Hot Tip:

Manage Results, Not Methods

Within the bounds of our Family Constitution, each family member is account-able for certain responsibilities and standards of conduct. Rewards and conse-quences get dispensed based on results, not the method of achieving them.

I don't want to have to manage when my kids take their shower or brush their teeth. That should be up to them. All I care about is that by the time they go to bed, they've completed all that is expected of them. If Jack or Max needs help, advice or reminders, Karen and I are happy to oblige, but only if asked.

We argue less with the kids under these circumstances, as we are not inter-rupting their shows or activities to force them to do something against their will. They manage themselves and make choices based on a very simple formula— get the job done right and reap the associated benefits; ignore responsibilities and suffer the consequences.

---

ily. An annual amendment process prompts us to look forward and antici-pate upcoming problems, rather than react to them after they arrive.

The *Constitutional Way* had been available to me all along. I just had to recog-nize it was there, then reach out and grab it.

POOPER SCOOPER

I recently searched the house for Jack to remind him to clean up after the dog. He hadn't gotten a Drop (our lingo for failing to complete a chore on time) for five consecutive weeks. He was closing in on his eight-week reward, a coveted opportunity to select a family outing. I didn't want to deflate Jack's efforts, as he had worked hard to maintain success. I wanted to help prevent a simple oversight from causing him to return to the be-ginning. I looked for him to give him a reminder.

As I called his name, he walked through the door. I reminded him to clean up outside, but he had just done it. He had used the checklist I had given him to remind him of his obligations. He wanted to keep his streak going. For the first time that I could remember, chores were *his* priority.

Chapter 4:

MY FAMILY'S CLIMB FROM ROCK BOTTOM

"A bend in the road is not the end of the road... unless you fail to make the turn."

—AUTHOR UNKNOWN

I didn't know what to expect from my family when I shared my initial vision for the Family Constitution. I felt certain we all wore the emotional scars from repeated battles and daily chaos together. I didn't anticipate open-arm acceptance, but the absence of curious optimism surprised me.

I tried to understand my family's cool indifference to a tool that could really help us improve the way we lived and interacted. I attributed their lack of enthusiasm to a combination of pessimism, confusion and fear. Truth be told, I didn't know exactly what their hesitation was. I just wanted to make us better.

THE FIRST ATTEMPT

I spent the summer of 2007 preparing for a chance to rectify my family's core problems: lack of *clarity, consistency* and *commitment*. I looked inside myself, observed our family dynamic, and spent countless hours drafting and refining our Family Constitution.

I recognized I had to be impartial and fair. The Family Constitution had to have enough appeal to generate genuine interest from my family members. I proceeded through the process by myself, keeping these goals in mind.

I finished my first draft of the Family Constitution with great pride and optimism in August 2007, three months after Black Sunday. I introduced it to my family. We talked about it at length. We smoothed out the rough edges.

We finally ratified our inaugural Family Constitution on September 2, 2007. Karen, Jack and Max tolerated the new structure at first; got used to it over the first couple of months; and eventually came to appreciate some of its elements. It made our household better, nobody questioned that. But, within my family, this initial attempt never generated the excitement and enthusiasm I had hoped for.

Live and Let Die

It eventually became clear that our Family Constitution needed an overhaul; so after nine months, I chose to let the First Attempt die. I wanted to remind my family why we needed boundaries. I needed to give them a full palette of issues to reflect upon during our next attempt. To me, we had to take one step back in order to move two steps forward.

With no official announcement, I simply stopped enforcing the rules over the summer. We slowly slipped back into old patterns. With wilted boundaries and absent structure, minor chaos returned to our home, but this time it was different. I had assumed the role of impartial observer. I watched the dynamics play out in front of me without the emotional responses I had previously experienced.

Prior to the Family Constitution, I colored my perception with fear and anxiety. I felt defensive because I knew I had problems that I couldn't solve. This time, the erosion of structure was a choice, an experiment, a demolition in preparation for new construction.

Whining and arguing returned, but not nearly to the same intensity. We had grown more tolerant and respectful of each other. We understood each others' needs better. Most importantly, we had learned how to enjoy each others' company.

To my pleasant surprise, one rule rose from the ashes. I routinely heard the boys use the "15-minute Notice" to join a video game. Was the survival of this rule symbolic of Jack and Max's acceptance of structure or was I blindly optimistic? I didn't know, but it gave me renewed hope. Despite the First Attempt's challenges, we would have a bona fide fresh start in the fall.

TAKE TWO

Take Two kicked off with me walking a fine line. If the Family Constitution were going to live up to its potential, I needed Karen and kids to devote their time, effort and thought *up front*. They had to help *design* our structure, not simply react to my ideas.

On the flip side, I couldn't afford further resentment towards our Family Constitution. Placing strict demands on my family and their time would certainly leave me short of the goal. I carefully calculated how to generate willing participation.

I turned to the power of food, an awe-inspiring force in my family. The kids and I began a ritual trip to Starbucks. Each Tuesday and Thursday morning, we went there to discuss a different topic. I drank my precious coffee. The kids ate their favorite pastries. We talked about the Family Constitution casually as we sat.

Recalling their lack of enthusiasm for the First Attempt, I hesitated to dive straight into rules and boundaries at our first meeting. Instead, I dipped a toe in the water. I chose my first words very carefully, "What *rewards* would *you* like to see added to our Family Constitution?"

Jack and Max each came up with a few modest requests. I added a few suggestions of my own. As the list came together, we openly discussed, evaluated and built upon each idea. Before I took my first sip of coffee, we had a full page of potential rewards to choose from.

At the following meeting, we tackled another attention-grabbing subject— "What things about our family would you like to change?" I wasn't sure what I would get, but was pleasantly surprised with the replies. Jack and Max each had real ideas about issues that affected them. Jack wanted the ability to decide when his hair got cut. Max wished Mom and Dad would stop embarrassing him in public. Both kids wanted us to turn down the volume on our bedroom television at night.

Imagine the irony of that moment. I habitually argued with Jack and Max about their bedtimes in order to keep them well-rested, strong and healthy. In an instant, I realized that the volume of our television had been inadvertently sabotaging my efforts all along.

The following week, we jumped into the touchy stuff. Jack, Max and I brainstormed about chores. Again the kids surprised me. Each rattled off numerous household jobs that they would accept, as well as ones they would prefer to avoid. I had been fooled by the difference between talk and action before; so I took their words with a grain of salt. Nevertheless, they spoke openly without whining or protest. I felt cautiously optimistic.

After a few breakthrough sessions, I asked the kids if they actually might like our Family Constitution. They looked at each other, then at me, as if embarrassed. Almost in unison, they both replied "yes."

SECTION 2:
YOUR FAMILY CONSTITUTION

Chapter 5
CONSTRUCTING THE FAMILY CONSTITUTION

"To put the world in order, we must first put the nation in order; to put the nation in order, we must first put the family in order; to put the family in order, we must first cultivate our personal life; we must first set our hearts right."

—CONFUCIUS

My initial blueprint for the Family Constitution consisted of my Fantasy Football template and a hazy image of family structure. I didn't know exactly where the pursuit of my vision would lead me, but I was excited to find out.

Official construction of our Family Constitution started with a morning walk. I left my home before the rest of the family woke up. I returned an hour later with only five written words. At first, I felt a little anxious about my lack of productivity. Then, the profound meaning jumped off the page...each word represented a step in a greater process:

1. **Introspection**
2. **Vision**
3. **Observation**
4. **Prioritization**
5. **Structure**

One step would lead me to the next. I just had to follow the progression, figuring out the detail of each step as I went.

My family and I often give credit to our Family Constitution's finite boundaries and incentives for repairing our household. But, I believe it was the process behind our structure that truly enabled us to diagnose our problems and find lasting remedies.

Your family can follow the same steps I did to design a Family Constitution of your own. You can apply clarity, consistency and commitment to your own unique set of needs and circumstances. You just need hope and faith that your family can improve, as well as commitment to making happen.

I will share each step of the Family Constitution process from three different angles:

1. **The Mission** summarizes the *purpose* of each step.

2. **Tales from the Gales** details my family's *experiences* and *results* as we went through each part of the process.

3. **Tips from the Trenches** encapsulate the important *lessons* we learned through trial and error, observation and luck.

Take my stories and advice for what they are— bits of my family's experiences. The merit and applicability to your family depends on your parenting philosophy, as well as your family's unique needs and circumstances.

As you go through each step, keep in mind:

The More the Merrier— Fight for your entire family's participation, early and often. I ignored this during the First Attempt, forcing me to start from scratch with Take Two. Everyone has wants, needs and opinions. It is your job to make sure that they all get shared.

Kids Share Ideas, Not Authority— Karen and I encourage our children to share their ideas and opinions; however, our household is not a democracy. As parents, we specifically reserve the authority to evaluate, approve and interpret each and every rule in our Family Constitution.

Step 1: Introspection

The Mission

Look inside yourself to identify your *own* personal values, family principles and parenting goals. Examine yourself in the context of your many different roles (i.e. dad, husband, coach, employee, friend, etc.).

You will use your findings to formulate a vision during the next step. At that time, you will share your personal revelations with your partner. For now, complete the exercise in private.

Questions to answer:

➤ What matters most to you? (i.e. love, security, respect, time, money)

➤ What are your greatest personal strengths?

➤ Where can you improve?

➤ What unique qualities do you offer the people around you?

➤ How do you prefer to interact and communicate?

➤ How will you ultimately judge your effectiveness as a parent?

➤ Do your choices support your priorities? If you haven't prioritized, now is a good time to do so.

➤ What are your family's greatest strengths and weaknesses, collectively and individually?

Tales from the Gales

Experience

For the first time in 37 years, I vitally needed a deep and comprehensive understanding of myself. I was a novice at soul searching. So, to stimulate introspective thought, I made a pilgrimage to most tranquil place that I had ever known, the San Clemente Pier. I felt comfortable and relaxed there—truly myself. There could be no better spot to unlock my own secrets.

As I drove the last stretch of road, morning fog shielded the end of the pier from my view. I arrived with a sense of purpose. I didn't know exactly how to get my thoughts flowing, but I knew I wouldn't be leaving until I got answers. I didn't intend to build our Family Constitution that day, or even process any ideas. I sought simple understanding, both of myself and my family.

I spent half a day at the pier, walking, writing and walking again. My pen seemed directly connected to my mind. I had no filter, no interruption, no cloud and no inhibition. Each nugget of self-understanding begged new questions. I kept digging. The future success of our Family Constitution became irrelevant. The investment had already paid for itself. In one morning, I knew myself better than I ever had before.

RESULTS

Some of my thoughts were too private to share with anyone. Others I couldn't wait to reveal to Karen. Certain ideas filled up pages. Others were fleeting and never made it to paper. It didn't matter. All ideas were welcome that morning.

I left the pier mentally exhausted, but with great clarity.

The **general conclusions** didn't surprise me:

☞ *My family's general welfare represented the most important thing in my life.*

☞ *I'd do anything to preserve our health and unity.*

☞ *Generally speaking, we were blessed.*

☞ *We could adjust and improve. In fact, we had to.*

However, as I dug deeper, my introspective efforts revealed new and **unanticipated truths**:

☞ *My choices often undermined my goals as a dad.*

I felt like a "Weekend Warrior Dad." In the early years after Jack was born, I focused on developing my career to provide for my family. I figured if I worked hard, I would advance and be able to better control my own schedule when I needed to. Unfortunately, I never slowed down long enough for control of my schedule to make a tangible difference. After several years as a parent, I still based many choices on work needs, despite the supreme importance of my family.

I had always wanted to coach my boys, but never volunteered. I feared my work would suffer if I escaped two or three afternoons each week. I routinely missed important events (i.e. kids' award ceremonies) because of "urgent" business meetings. I regularly left for work before light and arrived home after dark. When I got home, I usually wanted to be left alone.

In short, I had never become the dad I wanted to be.

☞ *My window of opportunity is now.*

I always knew deep in my soul that time was more important than money; however, years of professional conditioning and ambition had buried that sentiment long ago. With Jack approaching his tenth birthday, I could no longer afford to wait.

I had to develop our bond while I could. Once hormones and teenage priorities set in, my ability to connect at a meaningful level would be severely impaired. Beyond any changes to household structure, I had to make myself more physically and *emotionally available* to my family. I had to base my decisions and actions on true priorities, not the fleeting needs of a boss, partner, client or transaction.

In the wake of my introspection, I internally committed to becoming a different dad. I would use my self-understanding to bring my family closer together. I would finally focus on what mattered most.

Tips from the Trenches

Find the Right Spot— Find the place where you are truly yourself; a location you can access easily; a spot where you're relaxed and comfortable, where your thoughts can flow without interruption.

Focus on Yourself— As you drift off into thought, focus on the way you perceive the world and the people around you. Don't think about how you can change others. Search for your core being. Be able to articulate your discoveries to yourself, as well as anyone else you may choose.

Take Your Time— Introspection is a unique experience. Each individual moves at his own tempo. Don't hurry. Position yourself mentally and physically to engage in thought. Realize when it rains it pours. Don't interrupt the flow when you are on a roll.

Share and Encourage— If you have a spouse or partner, encourage them to look inside themselves. Support them through the process and convey the importance of self-understanding. If they cannot grasp your message, recommend they read this chapter.

STEP 2: VISION

The Mission

Understand your family's guiding principles. Establish clear and mutual parenting objectives. Create a cohesive plan to realize those goals.

Topics to consider:

> ➢ What traits do you value most in people?

> ➢ What lessons can your kids learn now?

> ➢ What lessons are they not ready for yet? When can you teach these?

> ➢ How can you best teach each lesson? (i.e. lead by example, set expectations via structure, school of hard knocks)

> ➢ Which negative influences would you like to shield your kids from?

> ➢ How do you intend to balance independence, experience and safety for your children?

> ➢ What habits can you encourage now to achieve certain parenting goals later on? (i.e. sports or music may keep them focused on healthy activities when they become teens)

> ➢ How do you envision your relationships with your children when they become adults?

Tales from the Gales

During our first decade as parents, Karen and I never discussed our respective visions for raising our family. We communicated well enough to work through philosophical differences, but we never had a plan.

As Jack and Max got older and the issues became more complicated, our respective parenting efforts began to slowly disconnect. Karen and I sent mixed messages to the kids. Frustration mounted on all sides. We needed a cohesive vision and a united front. Our Family Constitution represented that opportunity.

I started this step by crystallizing my own vision. I identified distinct traits that I would like to see in Jack and Max when they eventually transition into adulthood. I talked to friends with older kids to gain ideas and perspective. I peered into the future to understand what Karen and I could do today to prevent problems with our kids tomorrow.

With my half of the vision intact, I sought to involve Karen. I explained the nature of the plan I hoped to create together. Then I asked her to explore her own core values and aspirations for the family.

A few days later, Karen and I had the conversation we should have made time for years ago. We shared our fundamental parenting objectives. We talked at length about our views on role modeling, encouragement and discipline. We compared our definitions of parenting success. We put together a clear vision for our family that we could both support.

RESULTS

The characteristics that topped my list were: independence, self-reliance, integrity, responsibility and happiness. Beyond that, I wanted Jack and Max to enjoy life to its fullest and truly appreciate the opportunities it offers. I hoped my boys would be capable of finding love and would have the integral tools to make it last.

Karen put "trust" at the center of her vision. She explained "Jack and Max need to know they can come to us with problems…that we can help them find good solutions." Health, happiness and kindness rounded out her list of desired traits.

Through open discussion, Karen and I came to better understand each other's parental philosophy. We identified our family strengths, as well as those areas we needed to improve. We kept talking until we had bridged our gaps and clarified our mutual ideals.

Our coordinated vision ultimately boiled down to the following:

Important traits	❑ Integrity and trust ❑ Responsibility ❑ Happiness ❑ Inner strength ❑ Kindness and social awareness ❑ Gratitude
Lessons to teach:	❑ Organization ❑ Effective communication ❑ Courtesy ❑ Honesty ❑ Loyalty ❑ Commitment ❑ Money management ❑ Pride in work ❑ Sharing and contribution
Habits to develop and support	❑ Active lifestyle (athletics, music, etc.) ❑ Healthy diet and exercise ❑ Good hygiene ❑ Social interaction

Tips from the Trenches

Understand Each Other— Clarify, restate and ask questions until you fully comprehend your partner's points of view. Recognize that words such as trust, integrity and responsibility mean different things to different people. Use examples to affirm the intent behind each others' words.

Respect Opinions— Prepare to encounter contrary beliefs. Listen openly. Understand your partner's views *before* you respond. Recognize that absolute right answers don't often exist, only opinions. Talk through differences without passing judgment.

STEP 3: OBSERVATION

The Mission

Examine your family in the context of your vision. Identify *potential* issues and behaviors to address in your Family Constitution. Detect interactions that most stress your family relationships.

Don't seek to analyze behaviors or solve issues that you observe. Simply note your observations for further consideration. You'll break down and refine concepts later.

Categories to consider:

- ➤ Attitude (integrity, aggression, approach to adversity)
- ➤ Behavior (sharing, putting toilet seat down, manners)
- ➤ Budgets (clothing, entertainment, food, gifts, etc.)
- ➤ Communication (listening, tone, language, interrupting, telling truth)
- ➤ Coordination (scheduling and organization)
- ➤ Education (homework completion, grades, attendance)
- ➤ Friends (visitors, hanging-out, expression, curfew)
- ➤ Health (bedtime, diet, hygiene, activities)
- ➤ Heritage (cultural understanding, language, ceremony)
- ➤ Responsibility (chores, money, decision-making)
- ➤ Spirituality (religion, values, charity)
- ➤ Safety (driving, drugs and alcohol, violence, sexual activity)
- ➤ Technology Content and Usage (internet, cell phone, home phone)

Tales from the Gales

EXPERIENCE

Before I could frame the Family Constitution, Karen and I needed to identify the areas where structure could help us most. We decided to observe our family interactions for 30 days to provide a complete snapshot of our household dynamic.

I took the lead and purchased several small pocket pads. I carried a pad with me everywhere I went, both inside the house and out. As I observed my family, I jotted down notes and classified each into one of three categories:

> ➤ Valued Behaviors
> ➤ Discouraged Behaviors
> ➤ Behaviors Requiring Boundaries (i.e. Screen Time or Bedtime)

I didn't attempt to qualify, filter or understand my observations. I just watched my family, listened intently and recorded thoughts as they came.

Karen didn't want to carry a pad and pen with her. With her busy schedule, she couldn't scrutinize our family with the same keen eye. Nevertheless, she gave me a few ideas verbally and via email. She listened to my observations and helped to expand upon them.

Even Jack chimed in. He asked me to note recurring problems between him and Max, including putting away and caring for video games and cleaning up after friends.

RESULTS

Our collective observations yielded the following as *possible* issues to address in our Family Constitution:

Valued Behaviors	☐ *Academic performance*
	☐ *Chores and allowance*
	☐ *Clean-up*
	☐ *Effective listening and communication*
	☐ *Following instructions*
	☐ *Participation in organized sports*
	☐ *Planning and participating in family activities*
	☐ *Politeness*
	☐ *Sharing and taking turns*
	☐ *Telling the truth the first time*
	☐ *Volunteering*
Discouraged Behaviors	☐ *Bad manners*
	☐ *Hitting*
	☐ *Lying*
	☐ *Poor care of property (particularly video games)*
	☐ *Swearing*
	☐ *Whining, crying and complaining*
	☐ *Yelling*
Behaviors Requiring Boundaries	☐ *Bedtime*
	☐ *Diet*
	☐ *Exercise*
	☐ *Hygiene*
	☐ *Meal Preparation*
	☐ *Screen Time: quantity, content (television/video games)*

Tips from the Trenches

Don't Overlook You!— Use your Family Constitution to help fulfill personal goals (i.e. exercise, weight loss or stopping a bad habit). Identify the behaviors now. Then, establish appropriate boundaries and incentives during the steps ahead. You'll be happy you did and it will set a great example for your kids.

Don't Dodge Sensitive Issues— Contentious issues don't normally disappear when they're ignored. In fact, they usually become more complicated. Record all issues that you observe, even the ones you don't currently feel comfortable talking about. You can think through each observation during the next step and then decide whether or not to tackle it.

Get the Full Picture— Select an observation period that allows you to gain comprehensive understanding of your family's issues and circumstances. I chose a month in order to allow for a complete cycle. Depending upon the depth of your needs and current understanding, you may be able to adjust to a shorter period.

STEP 4: ORGANIZATION AND PRIORITIZATION

The Mission

Sort and prioritize your family's observations. Finalize a list of primary issues you intend to address in your Family Constitution.

Tales from the Gales

EXPERIENCE

I had purposefully avoided thinking ahead during the first three steps, reluctant to focus on resolution until I had a comprehensive picture of our issues. I had written several pages of notes describing the many issues our Family Constitution could address, but had no answers...yet.

After the observation period, I typed up my notes in their entirety. I placed each specific issue, behavior and interaction that I had noted into one of the following broad categories:

➢ Attitude and Behavior

➢ Responsibility

➢ Health and Safety

I then printed my notes and sat down at my desk with three highlighters. I read through each observation carefully and assigned priority with the stroke of a highlighter (Green=Yes; Yellow=Maybe; Red=No). I based my decisions on each observation's practicality, measurability, urgency and alignment with our vision.

Each of these topics met our structural criteria. Each would be addressed in our Family Constitution.

Results

The *green* observations represented the "absolutes." Concepts such as "Screen Time," bedtimes and chores met all the important criteria above.

These were the confirmed elements of our Family Constitution, the critical building blocks of our structure.

I further contemplated each *yellow* idea before reserving a spot in our inaugural Family Constitution. Issues such as sharing, diet and hygiene aligned well with our vision. However, these matters were subjective and difficult to administer. I had to identify manageable parameters before including such concepts in our structure.

Some *yellow* ideas such as athletics, family activities, cell phones and viewing content got cut or shelved indefinitely. These subjects didn't warrant firm structure. Karen and I decided case-by-case decisions on these issues would better enable us to implement our vision.

Red concepts got discarded because each contained a fatal flaw. Annual garage clean-up wasn't that important. School performance wasn't fair or feasible to monitor because Jack and Max differed by grade and academic standards. Polite manners were too broad and situational to build structure around.

The final list included:

Attitude and Behavior	❑ *Hitting* ❑ *Lying* ❑ *Sharing* ❑ *Whining, crying and complaining* ❑ *Swearing* ❑ *Yelling*
Responsibility	❑ *Allowance* ❑ *Chores* ❑ *Clean-up* ❑ *Meal Preparation*
Health and Safety	❑ *Bedtime* ❑ *Diet* ❑ *Exercise* ❑ *Hygiene* ❑ *Screen Time:*

Tips from the Trenches

Share, Ask, Share, Ask— People don't always readily offer their feelings and observations. This is especially true if they don't appreciate or understand what they are being asked to do. Don't expect everyone in your family to write stuff down, especially kids. Be patient and find a way to extract each person's observations.

Trust Your Instinct— Prioritization of subjective material requires gut feel. If you're "on the fence" about a particular issue, skip it for now. You can include it at a later date if you decide it belongs in your Family Constitution. You're better off choosing the few concepts that will enhance your family the most, rather than cramming your structure with more trivial objectives.

STEP 5: CREATING STRUCTURE

The Mission

Produce a detailed framework for manageable family structure. Convert "approved" observations and subject matter into quantifiable boundaries. Identify incentives for each boundary. Negotiate structure that everyone in the family can understand and embrace.

Tales from the Gales

EXPERIENCE

With our observations prioritized, I began work on the body of our Family Constitution. First, I created finite and measurable boundaries. I composed language to designate firm parameters for each subject, leaving blanks for details still requiring discussion (i.e."__:__pm" bedtime).

Next, I assigned specific incentives to each boundary. The boys had given me plenty of ideas to work with during our first Starbucks meeting. For each rule, I selected rewards and consequences that I considered both appropriate and viable. I tried to find the right balance to motivate good choices.

When I had completed the draft document, we sat down as a family to fill in the blanks and negotiate the fine details.

Results

Rather than detail our entire Family Constitution here, I will share how my family arrived at an important solution. In order to provide perspective and facilitate understanding, I'll first guide you through my family's history and experience surrounding this controversial matter.

Screen Time

Since we've been parents, Karen and I have both subscribed to the notion that excessive use of television and video games ("Screen Time") is detrimental to Jack and Max's development. We have tried many different ways to limit Screen Time. Until recently, we had always fallen short.

PRE-FAMILY CONSTITUTION

We first tried the "say and obey" method. For many years, Karen and I allowed Jack and Max to consume Screen Time unless we told them otherwise. Whining, crying and yelling ensued each time we told the kids to turn the television off.

Next, we tried an experiment. We allowed Jack and Max unlimited Screen Time in hopes that they would grow bored and move on. Unfortunately, the Screen Time lure kept their attention for hours at a time. The boys took breaks, but more often than not, they quickly returned to the comfort of the television screen.

Eventually, we reverted back to the "say and obey" system. Arguments returned with heightened intensity. We still hadn't found the right balance. Like so many things, no reliable structure existed in our family to support our parental goals.

FIRST ATTEMPT

The First Attempt limited Screen Time to prescribed hours (7:00am-10:00am on weekend mornings and after 6:00pm each night). No exceptions. It made sense in theory, but lacked practicality. Inherent inflexibility caused frustration and inconvenience.

After a month of living by this rule, we amended the Family Constitution to incorporate "make-up" Screen Time, allowing the kids to replace the Screen Time hours lost to early morning baseball games and other obligations. It seemed like the obvious solution.

Unfortunately, make-up hours created new controversy. Jack and Max often wanted to make-up their Screen Time at friends' homes. Even when done at home, we had no effective way to track the time. Despite good intentions, we simply couldn't monitor "make-up" hours.

TAKE TWO

I drafted Take Two with the determination to resolve our perennial Screen Time problem. Karen and I talked about what we considered to be appropriate limitations for television and video games. We established the following targets related to Screen Time usage:

☞ *One hour maximum during weekdays*

☞ *Three hours maximum on weekend days*

In addition, Karen and I acknowledged that under no circumstances would we allow Screen Time to interfere with other obligations (i.e. homework, chores, appointments, etc.).

After setting objectives, Karen and I shared our intentions with Jack and Max. We asked them a few questions and gauged their responses. For them, Screen Time flexibility took priority over quantity. They wanted to play games with their friends above all else.

I meshed our parental objectives with Jack and Max's expressed concerns. I drafted a new rule that I believed could satisfy us all. Today, our Family Constitution addresses Screen Time with the language in the box on the next page.

The rule above asserts our objective, but allows inherent flexibility. Karen and I can adjust based on circumstances (schedule, outdoor activities, weather, illness) without compromising the integrity of the rules.

SCREEN TIME

Purpose

To encourage active lifestyle and healthy hobbies by limiting Screen Time (television, video games & computer) to approximately one hour per day during school week and three hours per day on weekends.

Rules & Parameters

➤ No Screen Time shall be allowed during weekday mornings.

➤ During weekday evenings, Screen Time shall be allowed only after all homework and chores are complete.

➤ Mom or Dad can provide verbal warning that Screen Time is ending and set a timer for 25 minutes; Screen Time shall cease immediately when the timer sounds.

Consequences

➤ Each Ding (broken rule) shall result in a one-day loss of Screen Time.

Tips from the Trenches

Start with Rewards— Focus kids on the good stuff up front. Start the Family Constitution conversation by asking what rewards each person might want to earn. If you hit a bump as you tackle more contentious issues, revisit the list of rewards to reel them back in.

Select Incentives Wisely— Understand each person's "hot buttons." Formulate rewards and consequences that are fair and well-defined. I have provided a list of potential rewards and consequences in Chapter 8.

Be Specific— Design language to limit gray area. Establish finite parameters. Explore plausible outcomes and implications of each rule before you incorporate it into your structure.

Prepare to Deliver— Nothing erodes trust or respect more than broken promises. Follow through on *all* incentives. Amend ineffective rules as appropriate, but don't compromise the integrity of your Family Constitution by failing to deliver on an earned reward or consequence.

Plan Ahead and Articulate— Basic understanding of your own objectives and concerns won't necessarily enable you to express yourself clearly to your family. Prepare to present your thoughts and ideas. Your honesty and clarity will inspire others in your family to do the same.

Prepare to Compromise— Don't overlook the cooperative nature of the Family Constitution. The goal is to achieve structure that the entire family can embrace. Compromise opens doors to solutions by confirming commitment and expanding the range of solutions.

PUTTING IT TOGETHER

If you've completed Steps 1-5, congratulations, you've now built the foundation for your new household structure. You're ready to mold your structure into a personalized Family Constitution, a lasting reflection of your family's dedication and collective personality.

In Chapter 10, I've included a copy of the Gale Family Constitution, as well as a few themed templates (i.e. Pirate Code, Fairy Tale, Football Game Plan, and Castle Code). Use these documents to generate ideas on how your family can create a fun and effective basis for structure and communication.

Visit www.yourfamilyconstitution.com to download electronic templates, to enroll in a Family Constitution workshop, or to sign-up for a personalized coaching package to help with your journey. If we can help in another way, let us know how by emailing help@yourfamilyconstitution.com.

For more practical parenting ideas and resources, visit

www.yourfamilyconstitution.com
Parenting Resources · Workshops · Family Coaching

Chapter 6

LIVING THE FAMILY CONSTITUTION

"Feelings of worth can flourish only in an atmosphere where individual differences are appreciated, mistakes are tolerated, communication is open, and rules are flexible—the kind of atmosphere that is found in a nurturing family."

—VIRGINIA SATIR

Change is hard. New habits take time to develop. Communication barriers and emotional baggage dissipate slowly. Kids must test boundaries before they can respect them. I recognized these issues and knew our transition could not be seamless.

I felt caught in a quandary. I desperately wanted to avoid failure and resentment towards our new family structure. But at the same time, I couldn't compromise the integrity of our Family Constitution with loose or selective recognition of our new rules as we "warmed-up."

PRACTICE MAKES PERFECT

We decided to soften the adjustment with a trial period. During the week following official inauguration of our Family Constitution, we introduced our new boundaries without threat of consequence. We became responsible for satisfying the expectations; but, as rules were broken, Karen and I pointed out the "would-be" consequences, instead of enforcing them.

Throughout the trial period, Karen and I gave tips to the kids regarding time management and organization. We also used the time to identify and acquire supplies to aid our efforts, including clocks, timers, a weekly-planner, a bulletin board and storage bins.

By the end of the week, we were practiced and ready. We had familiarized ourselves with our new structure without resentment. We had adjusted to our Family Constitution without compromise.

FAMILY MEETINGS

Effective communication enabled my family to function again. During Take Two, we introduced a weekly Family Meeting to ensure we stay connected. It has become our forum to recognize achievements, address concerns, plan activities, coordinate efforts and discuss other important matters.

Our Family Meeting takes place each Monday night. If necessary, we'll reschedule to an *earlier* time; but we try never to skip or postpone a meeting. We attempt to keep the Family Meetings casual, brief and fun.

Everyone plays a role. Each opinion counts— but only if presented in an appropriate manner (no whining, yelling or crying). Each Family Meeting covers the same agenda.

We wrap up with family fun. We may play cards, Rock Band, Risk or Pictionary. If we've earned it, we might spend a night out at the movies, bowling or hanging out at Dave & Busters (a nearby restaurant and entertainment establishment). The place or activity we choose doesn't matter. The important thing is we do it together.

FAMILY MEETING AGENDA ITEMS:

Family Business	❑ *Issues and proposals*
	❑ *Topical chat (values, questions, current events, etc.)*
	❑ *Vacations and activities*
Weekly Planning	❑ *Dinners (each family member selects one "appropriate" meal)*
	❑ *Calendar (upcoming birthday parties, sports practices, business or social events, etc.)*
	❑ *Coordination (grocery shopping, rides to school and practices)*
Chores and Responsibilities	❑ *Review checklists*
	❑ *Acknowledgement and rewards*
Family Fun	❑ *games*
	❑ *movie*

BEYOND THE WRITTEN WORD: CLARITY, CONSISTENCY AND COMMITMENT

We couldn't possibly blanket every nuance of our family with firm and functional rules. An all-encompassing Family Constitution would be burdensome to create and even more difficult to maintain.

For many issues, time constraints and efficiency make the full "constitutional process" impractical. In some instances, the magnitude of a subject's impact doesn't warrant a spot in our Family Constitution. For other matters, the spectrum of potential outcomes may be too broad to effectively capture with absolute standards. For those issues not addressed in our Family Constitution, we still attempt to apply clarity, consistency and commitment.

Three C's and a Saxophone

In fourth grade, Jack played the cello to satisfy his musical requirement. Karen and I rented the instrument in good faith, but our investment quickly soured. We repeatedly had to remind him to practice. Jack complained each time; then proceeded to move slowly in order to minimize his actual playing time. I eventually became frustrated and vowed not to let this situation repeat itself.

For his fifth-grade musical curriculum, Jack had to choose between select wood instruments, wind instruments and vocals. I emphatically encouraged him to try vocals. Despite my advice, he selected the saxophone, the most expensive instrument available. I didn't want to compromise his "right to learn." Nevertheless, I felt reluctant to shell out money for another frustrating learning experience, particularly after I had vowed not to.

We talked through and resolved the situation using the "3-C's". I agreed to rent the saxophone for Jack. He agreed to practice on specific nights before watching television or playing with friends. Each time he complained about or failed to practice his instrument, Jack contributed $5.00 towards the monthly saxophone rent.

Today, Jack loves his saxophone. I can see his pride when he plays it. We didn't need to record the rule in our Family Constitution to make our agreement work. We just had to lean on clarity, consistency and commitment.

Ch...Ch...Changes

Change is inevitable. At a minimum, circumstances shift as kids get older. Some boundaries become antiquated. Others grow in importance throughout life's various stages. Whatever the impetus for change, structure must adjust to sustain effectiveness. I designed the Family Constitution to evolve with my family's needs and conditions.

We alter our structure via a prescribed amendment process. We solve small and immediate issues with *routine* amendments. We propose and ratify these simple changes during our weekly family meetings. In contrast, more complex and emotional issues require time, anticipation and preparation to resolve. For this reason, each summer my family tackles the "tough stuff" with an *annual* amendment.

Regardless of the amendment type, the adoption process remains the same. We discuss background and individual objectives surrounding a particular issue. Someone (usually Karen or I) proposes a solution. With all facts and perspective considered, we refine the idea until we find appropriate boundaries and incentives, or if we can't, we seek new alternatives until we find the right fit.

Usually, we come to consensus. In the absence of support from the kids, Karen and I can still affirm an amendment. Two parental "yes" votes mean we incorporate the proposal into our Family Constitution. One such "yes" vote means we keep searching for an appropriate solution.

Annual Amendment

The annual amendment process not only looks forward, but also reflects back. We flip through the calendar, mentally and physically. We recall past obstacles and anticipate upcoming issues. After identifying the topics, we discuss each as a family. Karen and I offer information and perspective. The kids enlighten us with their objectives and concerns. We take into account each opinion. Then we craft solutions before crisis and emotional barriers enter the picture.

Our attempts to look forward have yet to present many controversial subjects. Both my kids are still in elementary school. The issues on our immediate horizon are still simple. In a few short years, that will all change. We'll have to contend with thorny teenage issues: driving, dating, curfew, drugs and alcohol. By that time, we'll be well-versed in the annual amendment process and better equipped to cope with these major life changes.

Routine Amendment

If the annual amendment process is equivalent to a surgical procedure, the routine amendment process is like disinfectant and a band-aid. Routine amendments repair marginal rules and shore up relatively simple matters. Boundary clarifications, incentive adjustments and other small tweaks to policy all qualify as "routine."

Routine amendments occur as needed. They require only minimal preparation. Such changes can be presented, discussed and approved during the course of a weekly family meeting. Whereas annual amendments allow us to plan for the *future*; routine amendments enable us to better function *today*.

Routine amendments also serve to solidify oral understandings that couldn't quite stand the test of time. Verbal resolutions only work when all parties remember the same terms. When recollections of a verbal agreement vary, routine amendments establish written understanding to ensure confusion does not return.

BLUE SLIP BLUES

Karen, Jack and I verbally agreed that Jack would lose television for one day each time he brings home a "blue slip," a sheet of paper indicating he hadn't completed his school work from the night before. Jack determined that if he got the blue slip for a reason he deemed beyond his control (i.e. the teacher didn't write the assignment on the board) that he shouldn't have to miss out on TV.

After a couple of disputes, we talked about the issue at our weekly family meeting. We decided to amend the Family Constitution to include a rule stating "A blue slip received under any circumstances shall result in a one-day suspension of Screen Time." We haven't had to debate the issue since.

CASUAL KINDNESS AND CONSIDERATION

In my family, good decisions outside our agreed upon rules are every bit as important as those within. Karen and I try to acknowledge acts of kindness when we witness them, especially if no formal incentives exist to recognize the worthy deed. In many cases, we make special mention at a family meeting.

In addition to verbal reinforcement, we encourage Jack and Max to be thoughtful and compassionate human beings with "Casual Kindness and Consideration" tokens. We issue these when we observe outstanding behaviors, such as:

➢ Exceptional cooperation, encouragement or compassion

➢ Volunteering before request

➢ Unselfish decision-making

Tokens can be saved and redeemed for various prizes. In addition, the person who receives the most CKC tokens during the week chooses the game to follow our family meeting.

STAY THE COURSE

Don't allow panic or emotion to compromise the integrity of your Family Constitution. Impulsively changing rules to suit convenience impairs clarity. Adjusting incentives to reflect severity or intention spoils consistency. Without these elements, respect and commitment for structure will erode.

Realize that your Family Constitution will never be perfect. Understand that it may take time and adjustment to gain full support. Be aware that at certain points, even you may want to abandon the structure.

When in doubt, remember that your Family Constitution is a flexible utility resource. If a rule doesn't work, change it. Use the process to arrive at a better alternative.

Consciously avoid spontaneous adjustments and knee-jerk reactions in favor of thoughtful amendments. If you mess up because you are overcome by a wave of emotion, regroup and resume your quest. Learn from your mistakes and get better. The Family Constitution is about steady improvement, not perfection.

Chapter 7

HOUSEHOLD BILL OF RIGHTS

"Rights have to come from somewhere, and they come from community. In return, all of us have a responsibility to the community. Some people call this the 'communitarian' movement, but I call it common sense."

—RANDY PAUSCH

The U.S. Constitution has the Bill of Rights to define and protect the innate rights of human existence in our Country. The freedoms outlined in the Bill of Rights do not create opportunity. Instead, these liberties enable Americans to pursue their dreams and generate their own good fortunes.

The Household Bill of Rights echoes the same sentiment at a personal level. Jack and Max each deserve the tools they need to be successful. Whether they seek education, love, business accolades or all of the above, my job as a parent is to enable them. The Household Bill of Rights expresses the inherent privileges that the boys can rely on to find success, no matter how they define that nebulous term.

EARNED VS INHERENT RIGHTS

Earned rights require effort and commitment to be attained. Such privileges can be retracted when the recipient fails to uphold established standards. Drivers lose their licenses when they repeatedly disregard the rules of the road. Jobs get terminated when employees routinely show up late or ignore their responsibilities. Television gets taken away when chores are not completed on time.

Other earned rights don't get realized because the beneficiary never tries to realize them. The *right* to an education is meaningless for someone who won't register for or attend classes. The right to enroll at a prestigious university won't enhance a person's resume. However, a degree means something because of the knowledge and capability that such educational accomplishment implies. The effort behind the diploma carries the weight.

Inherent rights are unconditional. The U.S. Bill of Rights protects us even when we don't realize or appreciate it. These freedoms don't require effort or instruction to be redeemed. Likewise, intrinsic family rights, such as the "right to love" don't need boundaries and incentives to be realized. Instead, we convey these privileges through words, encouragement and deeds.

DELIVERING THE GOODS

The Family Constitution's rules teach earned rights. Its boundaries and incentives encourage effort and positive choices, the essence of earned privilege. To articulate and express inherent rights, I created the Household Bill of Rights.

I composed a list of the liberties that Jack and Max could count on. I didn't ask for their feedback. The gravity of such rights only comes with maturity and experience. Regardless of what soaks in, these inherent rights surround Jack and Max every day, protecting them in the absence of full understanding.

Karen and I will discuss the Household Bill of Rights with the kids each year, diving a little deeper each time. If Jack and Max can embrace even half of the concepts, over time they should develop into capable adults and conscientious citizens. At the very least, they'll always know that they have people who love them and support them no matter what.

Are the Gales perfect? Not even close. Emotional response sometimes causes us to slip up or lose our cool. Under such circumstances, Karen and I may temporarily ignore certain inherent rights. Nonetheless, reason always prevails to drive long-term solutions.

I composed the Household Bill of Rights from my soul. The concepts need little explanation to be understood on the surface; however, I couldn't find the rights words to express my sentiments. For that reason, I elected to define these rights through stories...

Right to Trust

"I'm not upset that you lied to me, I'm upset that from now on I can't believe you."

—*Friedrich Nietzsche*

Jack has always loved animals. From the time that he started to string sentences together, he constantly asked about getting a dog. I never wanted to add to the chaos of our house, so I continually denied his request.

When he was five, I decided to put an end to the incessant stream of pleas for a dog. I told him we would get a puppy, but only when he was old enough to take care of it. Nine seemed like a responsible age, so that's where I pegged it.

I'm embarrassed to admit it, but I secretly hoped Jack would forget. I suppose I was overly optimistic. For the next four years, I got a weekly reminder about my promise.

As we approached Jack's ninth birthday, I still vehemently opposed adding another living creature to our household. However, I had given my word. Despite my personal objection, I couldn't tarnish Jack's trust in me. I didn't want to set a poor example for him to follow. A month after Jack turned nine, we got a dog.

As an aside, I have really grown to appreciate how wrong I was. In Rusty, we've all found another outlet for love and play. He's family. I have also seen Jack grow and mature as he has taken care of Rusty. I am now truly glad that Jack's memory never lapsed.

Right to Ask Questions and Get Truthful Answers

"Don't make assumptions. Find the courage to ask questions and to express what you really want. Communicate with others as clearly as you can to avoid misunderstandings, sadness, and drama."

—Don Miguel Ruiz

Kids learn by asking questions. A few months ago, I brought home a book that showed classic LIFE Magazine covers. As I flipped through the pages with Jack and Max, we came upon a picture of the terrorists entering the Israeli compound during the Munich Olympics. Max asked who they were. I said "terrorists."

He wanted me to explain. However, I didn't know the how to describe terrorism to a six year-old. I sited 9/11, telling him that terrorists were the "bad guys" who flew the planes into the big buildings. I further explained how a different group of "bad guys" killed the Israeli athletes in Munich when I was a kid.

It may not have been the best way to answer his question, but I refused to dodge it. I felt Max deserved an honest answer, even if it was uncomfortable to discuss. I promised him that when he becomes a teenager, I'll tell him more if he still wants me to. He got the understanding that he deserved without the gory details. He also got a firm date when he can learn more.

Hot Tip:
Don't Assume Kids Know All the Facts: The Tourist Story

A few months after reviewing LIFE magazine and discussing terrorists with the boys, we all sat at my mom's house having dinner. As we talked about our upcoming vacation together, Max asked what we were going to do. My mom responded that we would be tourists and we could do whatever we wanted to.

Max's ears perked up and a concerned look fell across his face. "We're going to be tourists?" he said with a questioning voice. "Yes Max, we're going to be tourists" she answered. His expression changed from mild concern to confusion and alarm. "We're going to be bad guys?" he said with a perplexed voice. We finally understood his fear. He thought grandma had been telling him we were going to be terrorists.

Right to Learn

"When we send our kids to play organized sports– football, soccer, swimming, whatever– for most of us it's not because we're desperate for them to learn the intricacies of the sport. What we really want them to learn is far more important: teamwork, perseverance, sportsmanship, the value of hard work, an ability to deal with adversity."

—*Randy Pausch*

I never want to stand between my kids and life's enriching lessons. Whether it is formal education, sports, music or arts, if Jack or Max wants to grow, I want to help them. I proved this to Jack and myself before he had even reached kindergarten.

Jack's pre-school offered special programs for students to get acquainted with sports, arts, music or crafts. Each child was given the opportunity to take time outside of their normal day to play and develop skills with other like-minded children. When I found out that one of the options was "Ball Sports", I was ecstatic. Visions of me throwing him touchdown passes at our annual Turkey Bowl flag football game danced in my head.

When he opted for Ballet instead, I felt like my dream had died. I thought to myself: Why would my son choose Ballet over Ball Sports? Didn't he share my passion for football, baseball and basketball? Had he forgotten his first word was "ball"?

The selfish side of me wanted to encourage him to reconsider his decision. But, I recognized his right to learn. I would not dare stop him from moving in the direction he wanted. So, I enthusiastically asked about his progress after each class.

In the years since ballet, Jack has played football, baseball, soccer and basketball because those sports now interest him. Ironically, Jack readily applies the balance and flexibility that ballet taught him each time he takes the field or court for a game.

Right to Make Mistakes and Live to Tell about Them

"We cannot change the cards we are dealt, just how we play the hand."

—RANDY PAUSCH

Mistakes are part of life. We learn and grow stronger and more disciplined with each one. I wouldn't stop my kids from occasionally slipping-up, even if I could.

During my freshman year of college, my dad taught me to meet mistakes head-on with calmness and understanding. I embraced the lesson then and now try to apply it to my own family.

I lived in an on-campus apartment with three roommates. We decorated the walls with tiki torches, wall candles and life-size posters. A full-size volley ball net covered the ceiling of our "lounge." On a cool October night, we lit the torches and candles, but forgot to blow them out before we left for dinner.

We returned to witness the end of a major blaze which had ripped through our apartment. I called my dad to alert him to the situation. He heard my words, but assumed I was joking. I shouted "No Dad…I'm not kidding…" at least three times before the gravity of the situation sunk in. When he finally got past denial, he surprised me.

He first inquired about my status, letting me know his concern lay with my well-being, not the repercussions of my actions. He next asked how he could help. Not once did he get angry or reinforce my deflated self-esteem.

He allowed the natural consequences of my actions to teach the lesson. He didn't aggravate the problem by injecting emotion. Any residu-

al anger, disappointment or embarrassment he kept to himself, recognizing it would not help rectify the situation.

Not a Thanksgiving goes by that I am not roasted by my family for an event that is now 20 years behind me. With such a grand blunder of my own, how could I fail to understand my own kids' mistakes?

Right to Love and to Be Loved

"The most important thing in life is to learn how to give out love, and to let it come in."

—MORRIE SCHWARTZ

I think most parents and children would profess that they love their family. That being said, I don't ever want Karen, Jack or Max to have to guess how I feel about them. We may not *like* each other during every moment of everyday, but I've never doubted my family's mutual *love* for one another. That's what held us together during our trip to and through Rock Bottom.

Not a day goes by when I don't tell each person in my family that I love them. Karen does the same. More importantly, we show it through our actions. Even when Jack and I were drifting apart emotionally, we still expressed our love and need for each other. We consciously enhanced our relationship whenever and however we could.

We used our peaceful moments to throw the ball around or otherwise have fun together. We took "guy trips" each summer, enabling us to get away from our everyday grind. We used those precious times to remind ourselves of each other's redeeming qualities and our mutual affection for each other.

My kids need love to develop and stabilize emotionally. If everything around us crumbled, Jack and Max know that they are surrounded by unconditional love. Nothing is more important to me as a parent.

Right to Health and Safety

"If you have never been hated by your child, you have never been a parent."

—BETTE DAVIS

Kids don't realize it, but they lack perspective that only time and experience brings. Given the opportunity, Jack and Max could develop habits that would jeopardize their long-term health and safety. As a parent, my job requires that I keep them out of harm's way. Even when it's awkward or unpleasant, I always look out for their long-term health and safety.

I won't allow Jack and Max to eat whatever they want in order to quell argument. I can't stand by and let them watch television and play video games indefinitely simply to promote my own parental solitude. Such acts of selfishness would certainly make my life easier. But it might come at the expense of their ability to develop into balanced and healthy individuals.

Whether or not my kids know it, they *need* our help, strength and experience to safeguard their future. They have the right to develop into healthy adults even if they don't appreciate the meaning or intent of certain parental decisions.

I'll help Jack and Max to avoid bad habits whenever I can, even when it means pain and frustration to do so. I'll get to know their friends and help them steer clear of potentially detrimental situations. It won't be easy. My kids won't always like me. But, it's worth it.

Right to Follow Dreams

"As I see it, a parent's job is to encourage kids to develop a joy for life and a great urge to follow their own dreams. The best we can do is to help them develop a personal set of tools for the task."

—RANDY PAUSCH

The pursuit of dreams makes life worth living. My parents never held me back. I pledged to give Jack and Max the same gift. My kids haven't had the big dreams yet. Nevertheless, we can start with the "little dreams."

Max decided to play flag football at the tender age of seven years old. We had already been through this disruptive experience with Jack—ten hours of practice per week during the summer and six hours during the school year. Not to mention the travel games on the weekends. Nevertheless, Max passionately wanted to play.

I fought my selfish urge to steer him in another direction. Football was his dream of the moment. Crushing his ambition for a self-serving purpose would not only be unfair, it would send the wrong message. I want my kids to *know* they can pursue any healthy interests they have.

Max played and loved it. He got a few interceptions, a handful of tackles and all the lessons associated with disciplined athletics. He says he still wants to play next season. If he does, we'll gladly do it all over again.

Chapter 8

PRACTICAL PARENTING: IDEAS AND ACTIVITIES FOR TODAY'S FAMILY

"People seldom improve when they have no other model but themselves to copy after."

—OLIVER GOLDSMITH

Karen and I fumbled through our first decade as parents. We reflected on our own childhoods and observed other parents to help us navigate our way through various parental issues. However, I often felt as if we were re-inventing the wheel. I figured more experienced parents must have encountered and solved our same issues. Regardless, I felt unable to tap that collective wisdom.

I present this information for the sole purpose of stimulating thought and discussion. I have purposefully kept the ideas broad and disconnected to discourage the temptation to "cut and paste" as you create your own Family Constitution.

I designed our Family Constitution for my family's unique needs and circumstances. To realize the full potential of your Family Constitution, replicate my process, rather than my content. Build only on the concepts that suit your needs. Be creative. Try different combinations of rules, rewards and consequences. Find the recipe that works best for your household.

Commit now. Your solutions lie within reach.

RESPONSIBILITY

Few traits influence a child's transition into adulthood more than responsibility. Happiness, success and independence all hinge on this unique attribute. Responsibility can't be directly transferred or learned from a book. Instead, it must develop slowly over time through applied effort and experience.

Until recently, Karen and I had continually struggled to instill a sense of responsibility in Jack and Max. We couldn't figure out how to counteract a culture filled with convenience, unattainable expectations and immediate gratification.

Our Family Constitution enabled Karen and me to reset expectations and cultivate good habits within Jack and Max. We now have the tools to nurture their growing sense of responsibility. As the kids move closer to adulthood, Karen and I can monitor their progress and eventually let go, allowing life experience to replace parental guidance.

Chores

Growing up in my parents' home, my sister and I sometimes had to perform tasks that were anything but enjoyable. In hindsight, these jobs provided us with the chance to contribute to our family's overall well-being. Chores taught us that life is more than just a blind pursuit of personal indulgence.

Technology and low-cost/time-saving services have literally reduced the number of chores that need to be done in most domestic households. Dishwashers have eliminated need for traditional hand-washing, drying and stacking of dishes. Reasonably-priced carwashes can be found everywhere. Small yards, compact garages and inexpensive gardeners have turned lawnmowers into an oddity in many suburban neighborhoods.

Despite the lack of absolute necessity for kids to perform chores, I still feel the need to put Jack and Max to work. I can't bear to let my kids leave the house with an inaccurate sense of deservedness.

GALE METHOD

Karen and I had a couple of false starts when it came to injecting work ethic into our children. When Jack and Max were younger, we assigned them age-appropriate chores, and then insisted they comply. Unfortunately, we gave up each time because of the inconvenience to us. It proved to be much more work to monitor and administer the chores than to just do the work ourselves.

The Family Constitution provided Karen and me with the perfect chance to redirect our efforts. We now attach clear, consistent and escalating incentives to each assigned chore in order to encourage timely performance by the kids. Our Family Constitution outlines individual responsibility with the language on the following page.

Using this system, we reset Jack and Max's current expectations to include work and responsibility. To prepare them to gradually take on more, we provided advanced notice that they will assume additional chores and greater responsibility with each passing year.

> ## Helpful Hints: Chores
>
> *List Potential Chores*— Before you broach the subject of chores with your kids, note the areas where you most often request their help. My list included: getting newspaper, setting table, unloading dishwasher, vacuuming, taking out trash, wiping bathroom sinks, taking care of dog, and washing dirty clothes. I didn't intend to assign the entire list to Jack and Max. I simply wanted to ensure we had a broad palette of chores to discuss and choose from.
>
> *Think before Supervising*— Chores are meant to build good habits and self-esteem. Don't set your kids up for imminent failure. Select only those age-appropriate chores that your kids can perform *without supervision*. For me, this meant simple tasks for Max (i.e. get the newspaper, put away the silverware) and more advanced ones for Jack (i.e. wash and fold laundry, feed and clean up after the dog). As the kids get older, their chores will certainly grow with them.
>
> *Set Deadlines*— Establish reasonable completion dates and frequencies for all assigned chores. Start by defining how many times per week or month a given task should be completed. Then assign specific days for each. This will allow you foster routines, aiding success for your children and making your family structure easier to manage.

Under the Family Constitution, Jack and Max have become more self-reliant. They may not like some of the mundane work, but they accept it. They won't admit it, but their pride shines through each time we acknowledge another week of continued success.

Alternative Methods

The *Zone Defense* assigns "Chore Stations" or "Zones" to each family member. Each Zone consists of a series of related tasks. For instance, one person cleans the kitchen. Another completes all vacuuming and dusting. Yet another cares for the lawn and garden. The responsible parties complete all *daily* and *weekly* tasks required within their respective zones.

CHORES, HOMEWORK & RESPONSIBILITY

PURPOSE

To develop strong work ethic and encourage academic success.

DEFINITIONS

➢ Drop- any failure to complete an assigned chore or other obligation on time.

➢ Week- Monday to Sunday

RULES & PARAMETERS

➢ Each family member shall be accountable for completing his or her chores, homework and other responsibilities on time, as defined on the Chore Chart (See page 113)

➢ No television or video games shall be allowed until all daily chores and responsibilities have been completed.

➢ Chore Chart shall be reviewed at each weekly family meeting to assess performance by each individual.

REWARDS

➢ One week without a Drop:
   ◆ Full allowance (Jack- $8.00; Max- $5.00).

➢ Two consecutive weeks without a Drop
   ◆ Full allowance; and
   ◆ Sleepover with friend at our house or theirs.

➢ Eight consecutive weeks without a Drop
   ◆ Full allowance; and
   ◆ Choice of family activity.

CONSEQUENCES

➢ One Drop during a week
   ◆ Loss of ½ of allowance.

➢ Two or more Drops during a week
   ◆ Loss of entire allowance.

➢ More than two Drops
   ◆ Loss of television and video games for one day for each additional Drop.

The *Rotation Method* periodically shifts responsibilities among various family members. The swap may involve individual chores or entire Zones. Whatever the case, each person completes their assigned tasks for a finite period of time. At preset intervals, everyone involved in the rotation moves on to the next set of chores in the cycle.

Show'em How it's Done— Demonstrate each chore to your kids before having them do it on their own. Teach them how to be efficient and set clear expectations about the quality of work. After you've shown them how to do it, watch them do each chore themselves and provide instruction until they are able to do the work correctly. Not only will the jobs get done better, you will also eliminate the "I can't do it" argument from the start.

Keep the Chart in Plain View— In the interest of clarity and ease, my family's Chores and Responsibility Chart permanently resides in our kitchen. It hangs in plain view. Any of us can easily glance at it for reference or to check our progress. Routine may one day eliminate the need for reference, but seeing the chart reminds each of us of our obligations.

Allowance and Money Management

Financial habits ultimately leave a lasting imprint on lifestyle. Like math, music or athletic ability, some people have a natural ability to manage money well. Others must learn to be successful.

Before we release our kids into the world as adults, Karen and I would like to ensure that Jack and Max have good spending habits and sound financial sense. The Family Constitution allows us the opportunity to assess each kid's approach to money, then provide guidance where needed.

Gale Method

We first tried to teach Jack about money when he was six. We wanted him to start early, then learn over time how to prioritize value and make wise spending decisions.

So, we launched chores and allowance simultaneously. Unfortunately, Karen and I didn't clearly define the rules. We failed to effectively associate the money with the work, thereby dooming our lesson from the start. We promptly retreated to reevaluate our plan.

A couple of years later, Karen and I offered both Jack and Max the opportunity to earn money in exchange for performing specific chores (i.e. washing the car or cleaning the back yard). It was a good plan in theory, but unfortunately, Jack and Max had no clear motivation. Money didn't equate to purchasing power at the time because we restricted their spending. We told them how and when they could use their cash. A full piggy bank meant nothing.

The Family Constitution introduced a new alternative, as described in the "Chores, Homework and Responsibility excerpt on page 87. Jack and Max received allowance each week they completed their chores on time. If they strung consecutive weeks of success together, they could also earn a variety of other rewards, depending on the length of the streak.

Likewise, they faced escalating consequences when they didn't meet their

---

HELPFUL HINTS: ALLOWANCE AND MONEY MANAGEMENT

Always Make the Payroll— Pay allowances on time. Early on, I found myself without the right change on allowance day. Before we had a regular family meeting, sometimes I just forgot. The kids would float the question "Why should I do my chores if I'm not getting paid?"

Today, I stash my secret spot with a load of $1.00 and $5.00 bills, as well as a few roles of quarters. I replenish the allowance money well before it runs out to ensure I can always make the payroll.

Age, Allowance and Responsibility Grow Together- In our household, allowance increases with age and responsibility. As Jack and Max get older, they'll each be expected to do more work around the house. In return, they'll receive additional income to satisfy their ever-growing personal needs.

For example, at age seven, Max now puts away his clean clothes. When he's nine, he'll fold them, as Jack did at that age. Finally, at ten he'll be in charge of washing, folding and putting away his own clothes. His allowance will be bumped up each year to recognize the additional responsibility.

obligations. Since failure to perform did not excuse Jack and Max
from their respective responsibilities, they generally chose to reap full
benefit by completing their work as
scheduled.

In order to enhance commitment,
Karen and I stimulated Jack and
Max's need to earn money. After our
Family Constitution became official,
we stopped paying for "extras." We
no longer spontaneously indulged
Jack and Max with toys, video games
or snack food. If they wanted something, they could pay for it.

Jack and Max now distinguish between
Mom and Dad's money and their own.
They discern value and spend accordingly. They still occasionally ask me
to buy them something; however, I
respond to them each time with the
same answer…"How much money do
you have in your wallet?"

ALTERNATIVE METHODS

The *Investment* system provides kids with an allowance and a choice. A
child can either accept their allowance in cash or "invest" it in the Bank of
Mom and Dad. If paid currently, he receives the "face value" of his weekly
allowance (for example- $5.00). "Investing" the allowance defers payment;
but, like a real investment, the money earns interest.

$5.00 invested in the Bank of Mom and Dad may become $10.00 in six months.
This system requires that the "Bank" offers a very high "yield" to induce sav-
ing. 4.00% may be a great interest rate for a real bank account; but turning
$5.00 into $5.20 over the course of a year will not get most kids' attentions.

The *Allocation* method breaks up allowance into categories (i.e. charity, savings and spending money) and distributes cash based on a formula. A $5.00 weekly allowance may be divided-up as follows: $1.00 donated to charity; $2.00 invested in the Bank of Mom and Dad; and $2.00 put in the piggy bank. The key to a good learning experience is to channel enough money to the piggy bank to allow for meaningful spending decisions and to explain the significance of the portions that get channeled elsewhere.

INCENTIVES

Despite an infinite array of rewards and consequences to choose from, there are only a handful of them that get the job done right. The success of your Family Constitution's depends on your ability to recognize and deliver rewards and consequences that can effectively shape behaviors for each family member.

The summary on the next page provides ideas to consider and build on. Mix, match and modify ideas until you find the combination that best serves you and your household.

EFFICIENCY AND ORGANIZATION

Eliminate Clutter...The Easy Way

My entire family developed the bad habit of leaving things out when done using them. I made piles. Karen preferred concentric sprawl. Jack and Max just left things wherever they fell.

I eventually solved the problem with a trip to The Container Store. I bought four mesh baskets and disbursed them around the house. Today, anything that gets left out gets thrown in a basket. At the conclusion of each Family Meeting, we put the contents of each basket on the table. Karen, Jack, Max and I grab our respective stuff and put it away.

REWARDS

Prizes	❑ *Allowance ($)* ❑ *Books* ❑ *Clothes* ❑ *Favorite meal/dessert* ❑ *Hobby accessories* ❑ *Sports equipment* ❑ *Toys* ❑ *Video games and accessories*
Special Privileges	❑ *Car usage or subsidy* ❑ *Cell phone usage or subsidy* ❑ *Choice of family game* ❑ *Control of television remote control* ❑ *Extended "Screen Time"* ❑ *Individual time with Mom or Dad Night owl (stay up past bedtime)* ❑ *Sleepover* ❑ *Special interest lessons (music, sports, hobbies, etc.)* ❑ *Summer camp* ❑ *Time alone with mom or dad*
Outings: Entertainment	❑ *Amusement park* ❑ *Bowling* ❑ *Movies* ❑ *Restaurant* ❑ *Sports event*
Outings: Nature	❑ *Beach* ❑ *Lake* ❑ *Mountains* ❑ *River*
Outings: Adventure	❑ *ATV riding* ❑ *Boating* ❑ *Fishing* ❑ *Paintball* ❑ *Skiing*

CONSEQUENCES

Loss of Privilege	☐ Car
	☐ Cell phone
	☐ Privacy (i.e. remove bedroom door)
	☐ Television
	☐ Toys
	☐ Video games
Work/Physical	☐ Exertion (sit-ups, push-ups, laps)
	☐ Extra chores or tasks (clean garage, wash car)
Restriction	☐ Alone time in bedroom
	☐ Grounding
	☐ Time out
Other	☐ Early bedtime
	☐ Exclusion from activities
	☐ Fine

HELPFUL HINTS: INCENTIVES

Ask and Ye Shall Receive— Jack and Max told me what motivates them, but only after I asked them. I threw out a few suggestions to establish relative value; then listened as they listed the many ways they like to be rewarded. I used this information to ensure I got the most "bang for my buck" as I composed the rules.

Three Bears Rule— When Goldilocks visited the house of the three bears, she found three beds: one too hard, one too soft and one "just right." Take the time to discover the rewards and incentives that are neither too stringent nor generous. If you try incentives that don't work, try new alternatives until you find the "just right" formula that works.

Package Deals— Incentive bundles provide greater options and flexibility when searching for the "just right" combination. Combine various rewards and consequences to optimize motivation. Sequence and scale the assortment of incentives to persuade family members to continue good habits and terminate bad ones.

For example, Jack or Max can each earn allowance, sleepovers, movies and video games for completing their chores and other responsibilities. As they string successful weeks together, they move up the scale. Once they have established a good streak, they're motivated to continue.

Keep a Family Planner

To stay in sync, my family works from a common weekly planner. It sits in our kitchen and remains accessible to everyone. Each week, we record all vital information needed to stay organized.

I bring our planner to each family meeting. We review the past week to recognize performance, then plan and coordinate for the upcoming week.

Organization breeds efficiency. Karen and I know *in advance* who will be taking the kids to and from school, practices and other activities. We adjust meetings and appointments to streamline our respective schedules. We plan dinners for the entire week, so we only have to visit the grocery store once or twice.

Despite the fact that days are still twenty-four hours long, we have more time. We finally enjoy the peace of mind associated with being *functional*.

VITAL ORGANIZATION INFORMATION INCLUDES:

- ❏ School and activities drop-off/pick-up responsibilities
- ❏ Meal selections
- ❏ Topics to discuss at next family meeting
- ❏ Punishments (i.e. no television)
- ❏ Missed chores and responsibilities ("Drops")
- ❏ Social plans
- ❏ Vacations
- ❏ Birthdays, anniversaries, etc.

Catch Up Now!

Procrastination represents the universal defense mechanism of busy people. When faced with a time-crunch, we naturally defer flexible obligations in order to satisfy our most immediate commitments. We compromise our efficiency. We address minor problems at the expense of important ones. We create future crises in order to satisfy the demands of today.

The only way to ward off the procrastination bug is to catch up and stay current. I went to an office supply store and bought boxes, file folders, a label maker and all the other organizational supplies I needed. I started by organizing the eight months of filing that had accumulated in my drawer; then moved onto garage, closets and backyard.

Develop an organization method that suits you. Commit time to implement your method and maintain its effectiveness. If you have trouble committing, add the provision into your Family Constitution to motivate you to stay current.

Take Advantage of Online Efficiency

For many years, a mix of fear, procrastination and intimidation kept me from reaping the benefits of online commerce. I could have saved countless hours by simply by banking, paying bills and shopping over the internet. All along, I hesitated because I had convinced myself that time spent learning a new system would far exceed the amount of time I could actually save.

Finally, I dipped my toe in by paying recurring bills via my online checking account. Next, I moved to online shopping and e-business. I now realize I can do almost *anything* quicker, easier and cheaper on the internet.

FAMILY FUN

Find pastimes to enjoy with your family as a whole, as well as some to engage in individually with *each* family member. Don't settle for pursuits that amuse some participants at the expense of others. Strive to find the fun and games that everyone can take pleasure in.

Some of my favorite things to do include:

➢ Bocce with the *entire family*
➢ One-on-one basketball with *Jack*
➢ Football with *Max*
➢ Scrabble with *Karen*
➢ Risk with *Jack and Max*

We play the above games together with big smiles and open hearts. These are the precious moments when I love being a dad more than ever.

Below and on the opposite page are a few activities loved by both parents and kids alike. Once again, I'm providing food for thought. Let these ideas inspire you to generate a list of ways to enjoy your family. In the "Resources" section at the end of the book, I have provided a list of websites that can provide inspiration and access to many other family activities.

OUTSIDE FUN

Activities	❑ *Ball sports (baseball, basketball, football, etc.)* ❑ *Biking* ❑ *Fishing* ❑ *Hiking* ❑ *Paintballing* ❑ *Skating/Skateboarding/ Roller-blading* ❑ *Swimming*
Games	❑ *Bocce* ❑ *Croquet* ❑ *Horse shoes* ❑ *Paddle Ball* ❑ *Wiffle Ball (over-the-line)*

INSIDE FUN

Activities		
	☐ Arts and Crafts	☐ Model-building
	☐ Cooking and baking	☐ Wood-working (dog
	☐ Jigsaw puzzles	house, doll house,
	☐ Lego's	go-cart, etc.)

Board Games		
	☐ Backgammon	☐ Monopoly
	☐ Cards	☐ Pictionary
	☐ Checkers	☐ Risk
	☐ Chess	☐ Scrabble
	☐ Clue	☐ Stratego
	☐ Jenga	☐ Yahtzee

Video Games		
	☐ Guitar Hero	☐ Wii Sports
	☐ Rock Band	

HELPFUL HINTS: CREATING FUN

Look for Opportunities— Never stop the looking for ways to have fun. If you happen to be in a sporting goods shop, look for fun outdoor games. Likewise, search the displays when visiting a bookstore to find indoor activities and games. Finally, talk to friends and explore the many other ways families choose to spend time together.

Open Yourself to New Experiences— I never thought that I'd like sushi the first time I tried it. Now I love it. I figured playing video soccer with my kids would be somewhat of a bore. Now I share their passion. The older my kids have gotten, the more aligned our interests have become. But, even when they were much younger, I would try just about anything before discounting the potential for my enjoyment.

Give'em a Taste—Just as I try their stuff, I expose Jack and Max to my forms of fun. I've taken them to football games, the beach and other places I enjoy. They rarely want to go with me the first time; however, they almost never want to come home after they get a flavor for the fun. I've introduced ideas that have bombed too. But, I always make mental notes and return only to the good stuff.

Chapter 9

END OF THE BOOK, BUT NOT THE JOURNEY

"Continual improvement is an unending journey."

—*LLOYD DOBENS*

THE CLIMB

On Black Sunday, the climb from the depths of Rock Bottom appeared insurmountable. I looked everywhere for rescue from my family problems, unaware that the path to redemption stood before me in the form of clarity, consistency and commitment.

As my family raced through the summer of 2008, Jack and I spent a long weekend at the beach together. We arrived at our coastal campsite with the only essentials (tent, food, water, games) and a very loose plan. Friday morning, we pitched our tent. We then walked to the beach and had the time of our lives: talking, laughing, playing in the waves and setting a record for our new-found favorite hobby, paddle ball.

On Saturday, Jack and I went to war together at a nearby paintball park. We played through several rounds of combat. We fought in the trenches, advanced on the enemy team, and covered each others' back under fire. I almost always got shot quickly, inadvertently allowing me to stand back and admire Jack.

Bruised, sweaty and covered in paint, we returned to our campsite, then walked to the beach. We played bocce, launched our new surf kayak and recounted our morning paintball battles. We hung out all day…as buddies.

Jack and I didn't bicker once during our entire getaway. We returned home on Sunday morning, bubbling about the fun and excitement that we had experienced together.

On Black Sunday, the prospect of sharing such special memories with Jack looked remote. The notion that this good vibe could become the norm in our relationship seemed next to impossible. Our weekend together proved to both of us how far we had come together.

I don't contend that our healed relationship is perfect. Jack and I still argue. We still have our differences. However, we have identified the disease that plagued our relationship. We treat the symptoms with steady doses of honest communication. When we find ourselves at odds, we strive to find clear and consistent solutions.

Now, Jack and I genuinely want to spend time together. We play at the community pool. We throw the football. He even joins me on quick trips to the store sometimes, just for the company (and a doughnut). I feel like it's the way a father-son relationship should be. We're healthy.

My other family relationships are every bit as precious. These too have improved dramatically in the wake of our Family Constitution. We recently took a family trip to Pismo Beach, California. There we met my parents, my sister and her family.

Prior to our Family Constitution, rarely had I gone away with Karen and the boys without raising my voice. Never had I traveled with the extended clan without boiling over at least once.

Our trip to Pismo confined Karen, Jack, Max and me to a car together for four hours each way. Upon arrival, we shared tight accommodations with the rest of my family for three days. We roamed around Pismo and tried to balance the interests of nine people simultaneously.

In a true testament to our progress, we passed this formidable test with flying colors. I raised my voice only in excitement each time we set a new paddle ball record. We were relaxed. No one was defensive. We enjoyed each others' company. We were a functional family. It was awesome.

PARTING THOUGHTS

Before you close this book, I would like to take one last chance to remind you...

Make the Effort

"Garbage in, Garbage out" isn't just a cliché, it's a natural law that is as true as gravity. The Family Constitution can only be effective if taken seriously. It will only work if you make a real commitment to work through family challenges together. If you decide to take on the process, be judicious and diligent. Have faith that the effort you invest in the Family Constitution will pay off. Then make it happen.

Have Realistic Expectations

Taper your expectations. I designed our Family Constitution to *improve* my household dynamic, *not perfect* it. Engage in the Family Constitution process determined to make your family better. Establish a platform for steady growth. But, don't lose sight of the fact that the "quick fix" doesn't exist.

Enjoy Your Family

Finally, enjoy your family and relish the bonds. Time goes by very quickly. Remain focused on what's important. There are no "second chances" to enjoy some great parenting moments. If you are a new parent or a parent-to-be, it may be hard to recognize this crucial lesson at this time, but you will undoubtedly appreciate it in the long run.

Now What?

Thank you for taking your valuable time to journey with my family and yours. If you're reading this sentence, you've likely made it to the end of the book...but you still have work to do. So, now what? Relax, we are here to help.

First, review the copy of the Gale Family Constitution, as well as the themed templates, provided in Chapter 10. These documents will help you visualize the possibilities for your own Family Constitution. Just remember, these are Gale Family house rules, designed by the Gales for our unique needs and circumstances. Simple copy and paste is not a good option.

Next, take some time to try the exercises laid out in Chapter 5. Realize that there are no right or wrong answers. Improving your family takes time and commitment. Don't give up if you make a few mistakes, these are an integral part of the improvement process.

Finally, visit www.yourfamilyconstitution.com. There, you'll be able to access useful tools and templates, fun "Family Homework" assignments, and all the resources you'll need to make your personalized Family Constitution a success.

If your family would prefer a guided journey, then attend a *Your Family Constitution* Workshop, or obtain individualized advice during a *Your Family Constitution* Coaching Session.

If you have any other unique needs or circumstances, we are here to help. Please send an email to help@yourfamilyconstitution.com.

For more information on
personalized family coaching, visit

www.yourfamilyconstitution.com

Parenting Resources · Workshops · Family Coaching

WANT YOUR FAMILY'S RULES TO LOOK LIKE THIS?

See Chapter 10 for fun alternative templates

Chapter 10

GALE FAMILY CONSTITUTION & OTHER THEMED TEMPLATES

"Home is the place where boys and girls first learn how to limit their wishes, abide by rules, and consider the rights and needs of others."

—*Sidonie Gruenberg*

This book would not be complete without sharing the actual Family Constitution document that inspired me to write this book. I left this until the end in order to help you avoid the temptation to review what worked for my family before evaluating and processing your own family's needs.

If you're peeking ahead and have not yet finished the book, it's alright. I probably would have too; however, I encourage you to read the rest of the book before creating your own Family Constitution.

I've also included four alternate templates:

- Pirate Code
- Fairy Tale
- Family Game Plan (Football)
- Castle Code

These themed alternatives were designed for those parents who desire effective structure, but wish to add some flavor to the process to engage the kids.

More template designs can be found at www.yourfamilyconstitution.com. Or, if you would like us to help you pioneer a new template, email us at templates@yourfamilyconstitution.com.

Gale Family Constitution

We the Gale Family, in Order to create a more harmonious Existence, establish Justice, insure domestic Tranquility, promote the general Welfare, and secure the Blessings of Liberty to ourselves and our Posterity, do ordain and establish this CONSTITUTION for the Gale Family.

Article 1. The Basics.

SECTION 1.1. FAMILY MEMBERS.

The Gale Family shall be composed of five members: Jack Gale (kid), Max Gale (kid), Scott Gale (Dad), Karen Gale (Mom) and Rusty (dog).

Mom and Dad shall serve as Managers and executors of the Gale Family Constitution. Each shall strive to be *responsible, fair, just* and *consistent.*

SECTION 1.2. DEFINITIONS.

Ding - Broken rule.

Drop - Failure to perform chores or responsibilities *on time*.

Screen Time - Usage of television, video games, computer and hand-held games.

Week - Monday to Sunday.

SECTION 1.3. FAMILY MEETINGS.

Meetings shall occur weekly on Tuesday evenings. The ideas, interests and concerns of each family member shall be heard and considered, providing that they are expressed in a *calm* and *respectful* manner.

Each meeting shall cover the following topics:

Family Business
❖ Issues and proposals;
❖ Topical chat (questions, current events, etc.)
❖ Upcoming vacations and activities

Weekly Planning
❖ Dinner planning (each person selects for one weeknight);
❖ Calendar (upcoming parties, events, practices, etc.)
❖ Coordination (grocery shopping; rides to school and activities)

Chores and Responsibilities
❖ Review checklists
❖ Acknowledgement and rewards

Family Fun (games, movie, etc.)

Article *II*. The Rules.

SECTION 2.1. ATTITUDE & BEHAVIOR.

Purpose
To promote good decisions, as well as clear and calm communication.

Rules & Parameters
❖ Whining, complaining, yelling, and name-calling shall result in one verbal warning, followed by the escalating consequences, as described below.

❖ Hitting, kicking, or intentionally damaging property shall result in immediate Level 2 consequences.

❖ Lying or "parent-shopping" shall result in immediate Level 3 consequences.

Consequences
1. Five-minute time out;
2. One hour in room;
3. Twenty-four hours without Screen Time for each Ding thereafter.

SECTION 2.2. CHORES, HOMEWORK & RESPONSIBILITY.

Purpose
To develop strong work ethic and encourage academic success.

Rules & Parameters
❖ Each family member shall be accountable for completing his or her chores, homework and other responsibilities on time, as defined on the Chore Chart.

❖ No television or video games shall be allowed until all daily chores and responsibilities have been completed.

❖ Chore Chart shall be reviewed at each weekly family meeting to assess performance by each individual.

Rewards

❖ Each week without a Drop: Full allowance (Jack- $8.00; Max- $5.00).

❖ Four consecutive weeks without a Drop:
Sleepover with friend at our house or theirs.

Consequences

❖ One Drop during a week: Loss of ½ of allowance.

❖ Two or more Drops during a week: Loss of entire allowance.

❖ More than two Drops: Loss of Screen Time for one day for
each additional Drop.

SECTION 2.3. SCREEN TIME.

Purpose

To encourage active lifestyle and
healthy hobbies by limiting Screen
Time to approximately one hour per
day during school week and three
hours per day on weekends.

Rules & Parameters

❖ No Screen Time shall be allowed during weekday mornings.

❖ During weekday evenings, Screen Time shall be allowed only after all homework
and chores are complete.

❖ Mom or Dad can provide verbal warning that Screen Time is ending and set a
timer for 25 minutes; Screen Time shall cease immediately when the timer sounds.

Consequences

❖ Each Ding shall result in a one-day loss of Screen Time.

SECTION 2.4. BEDTIME.

Purpose
To develop healthy sleep habits.

Rules & Parameters
❖ Jack and Max shall be individually responsible for being ready for bed, including brushed teeth, by their assigned bed time (Max- 8:30pm; Jack- 9:15pm).
❖ If circumstances require Jack or Max to stay up past their bed time, each shall be prepared for bed within 15 minutes of arriving home.

Rewards
❖ If Jack or Max makes it to bed on time each night between Sunday and Thursday, then he can stay up until 10:00pm on Friday and Saturday nights.

Consequences
❖ Each Bedtime Ding shall result in a bedtime thirty minutes earlier the following night.

SECTION 2.5. MEALS & NUTRITION.

Purpose
To develop good eating habits, simplify meal preparation, and encourage self-sufficiency.

Rules & Parameters
Breakfast, Lunch, Snacks
❖ Jack and Max shall be responsible for preparing their own breakfasts, lunches and snacks, unless Mom or Dad offers.
❖ Each family member shall choose one healthy dinner meal per week.
❖ If someone chooses not to eat a prepared dinner, he or she can prepare an alternative meal for themselves (i.e bread & butter, left-overs, etc.).
❖ Dessert shall be available only to kids who eat enough dinner, as determined by Mom or Dad.

SECTION 2.6. PERSONAL HYGIENE

Purpose
To promote health and cleanliness.

Rules & Parameters
❖ Jack and Max shall each be responsible for getting himself dressed in *clean* clothes every day.
❖ Jack and Max shall shower every morning before school; alternatively, they can bathe the night before.

Consequences
❖ First Personal Hygiene Ding shall result in a warning.
❖ Each Personal Hygiene Ding thereafter shall result in a one-day loss of Screen Time.

Article *III.* Process and Authority.

SECTION 3.1. AMENDMENTS.

Mom *and* Dad must both approve each amendment to the Family Constitution before it can take effect.

Amendments can be proposed, considered and approved during weekly Family Meeting.

SECTION 3.2. RATIFICATION.

The Ratification of the Gale Family Constitution shall occur upon the understanding and signature of all Members of the Gale Family.

On this ____ day of _____ ,We the Members of the Gale Family hereby ratify the Gale Family Constitution of 2008.

Scott Gale _____

Karen Gale _____

Jack Gale _____

Max Gale _____

Chores & Responsibilities	Scott	Karen	Jack	Max	M	T	W	Th	F	Sa	Su
FALL 2009					For The Week Of:						
Cook Dinner	x	x									
Load/Unload Dishes	x										
Pick up/Drop-off Kids at School	x										
Wash & Fold Laundry		x									
Refill Toilet Rolls/ Paper Towels			x								
Dishwasher-Put Away Silverware			x								
Rusty - Feeding (daily)			x								
Rusty - Poop Pick-up (T, Th, Sat)			x								
Turn-off All Lights (weekday am)			x								
Set Table (daily)				x							
Get Newspaper (daily)				x							

Want your family's rules to be fun, meaningful, clear and consistent?

Want to communicate effectively as a family, and focus on what matters most as a parent?

Create your own Family Constitution with one of our fun templates. Display it proudly today and look back on it fondly tomorrow.

Visit www.yourfamilyconstitution.com for more information.

Please allow us to help you help your family. We've got a wide variety of templates to suit your family's unique personality and interests.

Visit **www.yourfamilyconstitution.com** *to see our newest templates. If we don't have the theme you're looking, we'll customize one for you.*

Paint your pirate ship... discover buried family treasure!

Pirate's Code

Pirate's Code

Aye... journey to the Pirate's Cove with me to find the buried treasure. Board me ship, meet me crew. We've got a lot of pirate work to do.

Captain & Crew
- Captain Scott (Dad)
- First Mate Karen (Mom)
- Jack the Joker (Crew)
- Mighty Max (Crew)

DEFINITIONS

Cannonball - Broken rule.

Black Spot - Failure to perform chores or responsibilities on time.

Screen Time - Usage of television, video games, computer and hand-held games.

Week - Monday to Sunday.

All-Hands-On-Deck Gathering - Tuesday evening meetings. All ships crew shall listen, show respect, and provide ideas on how to improve the ship.

CODE OF CONDUCT

ARTICLE ONE. ATTITUDE & BEHAVIOR

Pirate Conduct
- ✖ Whining, complaining, yelling, and name-calling shall result in one verbal warning, followed by the Deadman's Curses below.
- ✖ Hitting, kicking, or damaging other people's stuff shall result in immediate Level 2 Deadman's Curses.
- ✖ Lying or parent-shopping shall result in immediate Level 3 Deadman's Curses.

Deadman's Curses
1. Five-minute time out;
2. One hour in room;
3. Twenty-four hours without Screen Time for 3rd Cannonball and each thereafter.

ARTICLE TWO. CHORES, HOMEWORK & RESPONSIBILITY

Pirate Conduct

✖ Each family member shall be accountable for completing his chores, homework and other responsibilities on time, as defined on the Chore Chart.

✖ No television or video games shall be allowed until all daily chores and responsibilities have been completed.

✖ Chore Chart shall be reviewed at each weekly family meeting to assess performance by each individual.

Jewels

✖ Each week without a Black Spot -
Full allowance

✖ Four consecutive weeks without a Black Spot
- Sleepover with friend at our house or theirs.

Deadman's Curses

✖ One Black Spot during a week - Loss of 1/2 allowance.

✖ Two or more Black Spots during a week - Loss of entire allowance.

✖ Each additional Black Spot - Loss of Screen Time for one-day.

ARTICLE THREE. SCREEN TIME

Pirate Conduct

✖ No Screen Time shall be allowed during weekday mornings.

✖ During weekday evenings, Screen Time shall be allowed only after all homework and chores are complete.

✖ At any time, Captain or First Mate can provide verbal warning that Screen Time is ending and set a timer for 25 minutes; Screen Time shall cease immediately when the timer sounds.

Deadman's Curses

✖ Each Cannonball shall result in a one-day loss of Screen Time.

MATEY MATTERS

BEDTIME
✖ Crew shall be individually responsible for being ready for bed, including brushed teeth, by their assigned bedtimes. (Max-8:30pm; Jack-9:15pm).

✖ If circumstances require crew to stay up past their bed time, each shall be prepared for bed within 15 minutes of arriving home.

Jewels
✖ If crew makes it to bed on time each night between Sunday and Thursday, he can stay up until 10:00pm on Friday and Saturday night.

Deadman's Curses
✖ Each Bedtime Cannonball shall result in a bedtime 30 minutes earlier the following night.

MEALS & NUTRITION
✖ Crew shall be responsible for preparing their own breakfasts, lunches and snacks, unless Captain or First Mate offers to help.

✖ Each crew member shall choose one healthy dinner meal per week for the family.

✖ If someone chooses not to eat dinner, he or she can prepare an alternative meal for themselves (i.e. bread & butter, left-over's, etc.).

✖ Dessert shall be available only to kids who eat enough dinner, as determined by Captain or First Mate.

PERSONAL HYGIENE
✖ Each Crew shall be responsible for getting himself dressed in clean clothes every day.

✖ Crew memebers shall shower every morning before school; or they can bathe the night before.

Deadman's Curses
✖ First Cannonball shall result in a warning.

✖ Each Cannonball thereafter shall result in a one-day loss of Screen Time.

HOIST THE COLORS!

Captain and First Mate must both approve each change before it can take effect. Changes can be proposed, considered and approved during any weekly All-Hands On-Deck-Gathering.

On this _____ day of _____,

The Pirate Code of Conduct is approved.

Captain _____

1st Mate _____

Crew 1 _____

Crew 2 _____

Construct your crown...
display the gems of
family togetherness.

Fairy Tale

Fairy Tale

Once upon a time, in a land not so far away, there lived...

- **The Jolly Giant (Dad)**
- **Mother Goose (Mom)**
- **Prince Jack**
- **Prince Max**

Definitions

Broken Arrow - Broken rule.

Poison Apple - Failure to perform chores or responsibilities on time.

Magic Screen - Usage of television, video games, computer and hand-held games.

Week - Monday to Sunday.

Magic Meeting - Tuesday evening meetings. All princes shall listen, show respect, and provide ideas on how to improve the Kingdom.

Sorcerer's Spell Book

CHAPTER 1. ATTITUDE & BEHAVIOR

Magic Spells

✳Whining, complaining, yelling, and name-calling shall result in one verbal warning, followed by the Curses below.

✳Hitting, kicking, or intentionally damaging other people's stuff shall result in immediate Level 2 Curses.

✳Lying or parent-shopping shall result in immediate Level 3 Curses.

Curses

1. Five-minute timeout;
2. One hour in room;
3. Twenty-four hours without Magic Screen for each Broken Arrow thereafter.

CHAPTER 2. CHORES, HOMEWORK & RESPONSIBILITY

Magic Spells
✴Each fairy tale family member shall be accountable for completing their chores, homework and other responsibilities on time, as defined on the Chore Chart.
✴No magic screen shall be allowed until all daily chores are done.
✴Chore Chart shall be reviewed at each weekly family meeting to assess performance by each individual.

Charms
✴Each week without a Poison Apple - Full allowance
✴Four consecutive weeks without a Poison Apple - Sleepover with friend at our house or theirs.

Curses
✴One Poison Apple during a week - Loss of 1/2 of allowance.
✴Two or more Poison Apples during a week - Loss of entire allowance.
✴Each additional Poison Apple - Loss of Magic Screen for one-day.

CHAPTER 3. MAGIC SCREEN.

Magic Spells
✴No Magic Screen shall be allowed during weekday mornings.
✴During weekday evenings, Magic Screen shall be allowed only after all homework and chores are complete.
✴At any time, Mother Goose or Jolly Giant can provide verbal warning that Magic Screen is ending and set a timer for 25 minutes; Magic Screen shall cease immediately when the timer sounds.

Curses
✴Each Broken Arrow shall result in a one-day loss of Magic Screen.

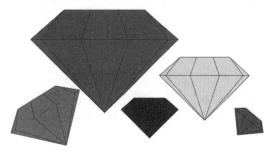

Magic Castle

BEDTIME

Magic Spells
* Princes shall be responsible for being ready for bed, including brushed teeth, by their assigned bedtimes (Max- 8:30pm; Jack- 9:15pm).
* If circumstances require princes to stay up past their bedtime, each shall be prepared for bed within 15 minutes of arriving home.

Charms
* If a prince makes it to bed on time each night between Sunday and Thursday, he can stay up until 10:00 pm on Friday and Saturday night.

Curses
* Each Bedtime Broken Arrow shall result in a bedtime 30 minutes earlier the following night.

MEALS & NUTRITION

Magic Spells
* Princes shall be responsible for preparing own breakfasts, lunches & snacks, unless Mother Goose or Jolly Giant offers to help.
* Each fairy tale family member shall choose one healthy dinner meal per week for family.
* If someone chooses not to eat a prepared dinner, he or she can prepare an alternative meal for themselves (i.e. bread & butter, left-over's, etc.).
* Dessert shall be available only to princes who eat enough dinner, as determined by Mother Goose or Jolly Giant.

PERSONAL HYGIENE

Magic Spells
* Princes shall each be responsible for getting himself dressed in clean clothes every day.
* Princes shall shower every morning before school; alternatively, they can bathe the night before.

Curses
* One Broken Arrow shall result in a warning.
* Each Broken Arrow thereafter shall result in the loss of Magic Screen for one day.

Fairy Godmother's Magic Wand

Mother Goose and Jolly Giant must both approve each change to the SORCERER'S SPELL BOOK or MAGIC CASTLE rules before it can take effect. Changes can be proposed, considered and approved during any weekly Magic Meeting.

On this _____ day of _____,

The SORCERER'S SPELL BOOK is approved.

Jolly Giant _____

Mother Goose _____

Prince _____

Prince _____

Create your team logo... Play hard and tackle the family challenges that stand before you.

Family
Game Plan

Family Game Plan

HOME FIELD
Coaches & Players
- Coach (Dad)
- Coach (Mom)
- Player #11 (Jack)
- Player #8 (Max)

DEFINITIONS

Fumble - Broken rule.

Dropped Pass - Failure to perform chores or responsibilities on time.

Big Screen - Usage of television, video games, computer and hand-held games.

Week - Monday to Sunday.

Huddles - Tuesday evenings meetings. All players shall listen, show respect, and provide ideas on how to improve the team.

Scoreboard - Chore chart.

PLAYBOOK

1st DOWN. ATTITUDE & BEHAVIOR
Plays

✔ Whining, complaining, yelling, and name-calling shall result in one verbal warning, followed by the Penalties below.

✔ Hitting, kicking, or damaging other people's stuff shall result in immediate Level 2 Penalties.

✔ Lying or parent-shopping shall result in immediate Level 3 Penalties.

Penalties

1. Five-minute time out;
2. One hour in room;
3. Twenty-four hours without Big Screen for each Fumble thereafter.

2nd DOWN. CHORES, HOMEWORK & RESPONSIBILITY

Plays
- ✔ Each family member shall be accountable for completing his or her chores, homework and other responsibilities on time, as defined on the Scoreboard.
- ✔ No Big Screen shall be allowed until all daily chores and responsibilities have been completed.
- ✔ Scoreboard shall be reviewed at each weekly Huddle to assess performance by each individual.

Points Scored
- ✔ One week without a Dropped Pass - Full allowance
- ✔ Four consecutive weeks without a Dropped Pass - Sleepover with friend at our house or theirs'.

Penalties
- ✔ Each Dropped Pass during a week - Loss of 1/2 allowance.
- ✔ Two or more Dropped Passs during a week - Loss of entire allowance.
- ✔ Each additional Dropped Pass - Loss of Big Screen for one-day.

3rd DOWN. BIG SCREEN

Plays
- ✔ No Big Screen shall be allowed during weekday mornings.
- ✔ During weekday evenings, Big Screen shall be allowed only after all homework and chores are complete.
- ✔ At any time, Coaches can provide verbal warning that Big Screen is ending and set a timer for 25 minutes; Big Screen shall cease immediately when the timer sounds.

Penalties
- ✔ Each Big Screen Fumble shall result in a one-day loss of Big Screen.

LOCKER ROOM

BEDTIME
Plays
✔ Players shall be individually responsible for being ready for bed, including brushed teeth, by their assigned bedtimes. (Max- 8:30pm; Jack- 9:15pm).
✔ If circumstances require players to stay up past their bedtime, each shall be prepared for bed within 15 minutes of arriving home.

Points Scored
✔ If players makes it to bed on time each night between Sunday and Thursday, then they can stay up until 10:00pm on Friday and Saturday night.

Penalties
✔ Each Bedtime Fumble shall result in a bedtime 30 minutes earlier the following night.

MEALS & NUTRITION
Plays
✔ Players shall be responsible for preparing their own breakfasts, lunches and snacks, unless Coaches offer to help.
✔ Each family member shall choose one healthy dinner meal per week for family.
✔ If someone chooses not to eat dinner, he or she can prepare an alternative meal for themselves (i.e. bread & butter, left-over's, etc.).
✔ Dessert shall be available to players who eat enough dinner, as determined by Coaches.

PERSONAL HYGIENE
Plays
✔ Players shall each be responsible for getting himself dressed in clean clothes every day.
✔ Players shall shower every morning before school; alternatively, they can bathe the night before.

Penalties
✔ First Fumble shall result in a warning.
✔ Each Fumble thereafter shall result in a one-day loss of Big Screen.

AUDIBLES

Coaches must both approve each change before it can take effect. Changes can be proposed, considered and approved during any weekly Huddle.

On this _____ day of _____,

The Gale Family Game Plan is approved.

Coach   _____

Coach   _____

Players #11 _____

Players #8   _____

Design your family crest...

Live well. Defend your

castle against all who

challenge its honor.

Castle Code

Castle Code

Hear ye... hear ye... come one and come all to the Kingdom of Gale

Royal Court
- King (Dad)
- Queen (Mom)
- Court Jester Jack
- Court Jester Max

Definitions

Broken Arrow - Broken rule.

Dropped Lance - Failure to perform chores or responsibilities on time.

Magic Theater - Usage of television, video games, computer and hand-held games.

Week - Monday to Sunday.

Round Table - Tuesday evening meetings. All members of the Royal Court shall listen, show respect, and provide ideas on how to improve the Kingdom.

King's Law

KING'S LAW 1. ATTITUDE & BEHAVIOR.

Royal Rules
✶ Whining, complaining, yelling, and name-calling shall result in one verbal warning, followed by the Curses below.

✶ Hitting, kicking, or intentionally damaging other people's stuff shall result in immediate Level 2 Curses.

✶ Lying or parent-shopping shall result in immediate Level 3 Curses.

Curses
1. Five-minute time out;
2. One hour in room;
3. Twenty-four hours without Magic Theater for each Broken Arrow thereafter.

KING'S LAW 2. CHORES, HOMEWORK & RESPONSIBILITY.

Royal Rules

✳ All members of the Royal Court shall be accountable for completing his or her chores, homework and other responsibilities on time, as defined on the Chore Chart.

✳ No Magic Theater shall be allowed until all daily chores and responsibilities have been completed.

✳ Chore Chart shall be reviewed at each weekly family meeting to assess performance by each individual.

Enchantments

✳ Each week without a Dropped Lance - Full allowance

✳ Four consecutive weeks without a Dropped Lance - Sleepover with friend at our house or theirs.

Curses

✳ One Dropped Lance during a week - Loss of 1/2 allowance.

✳ Two or more Dropped Lances during a week - Loss of entire allowance.

✳ Each additional Dropped Lance - Loss of Magic Theater for one-day.

KING'S LAW 3. MAGIC THEATER

Royal Rules

✳ No Magic Theater shall be allowed during weekday mornings.

✳ During weekday evenings, Magic Theater shall be allowed only after all homework and chores are complete.

✳ At any time, King or Queen can provide verbal warning that Magic Theater is ending and set a timer for 25 minutes; Magic Theater shall cease immediately when the timer sounds.

Curses

✳ Each Magic Theater Broken Arrow shall result in a one-day loss of Magic Theater.

Castle Customs

BEDTIME

✳ Each prince shall be responsible for being ready for bed, including brushed teeth, by his assigned bedtime. (Prince Max- 8:30pm; Prince Jack- 9:15pm).

✳ If circumstances require princes to stay up past their bedtime, each shall be prepared for bed within 15 minutes of arriving home.

Enchantments

✳ If a prince makes it to bed on time each night between Sunday and Thursday, then he can stay up until 10:00pm on Friday and Saturday night.

Curses

✳ Each Bedtime Broken Arrow shall result in a bedtime 30 minutes earlier the following night.

MEALS & NUTRITION

✳ Each prince shall be responsible for preparing their own breakfasts, lunches and snacks, unless King or Queen offers to help.

✳ Each family member shall choose one healthy dinner meal per week for the family.

✳ If a prince chooses not to eat a prepared dinner, he can prepare an alternative meal for himself (i.e. bread & butter, left-over's, etc.).

✳ Dessert shall be available only to princes who eat enough dinner, as determined by King or Queen.

PERSONAL HYGIENE

✳ Each prince shall each be responsible for getting himself dressed in clean clothes every day.

✳ Each prince shall shower every morning before school; or they can bathe the night before.

Curses

✳ First Broken Arrow shall result in a warning.

✳ Each Broken Arrow thereafter shall result in a one-day loss of Magic Theater.

Merlin's Magic Wand

King and Queen must both approve each change to THE CASTLE CODE before it can take effect. Changes can be proposed, considered and approved during any weekly Round Table gathering.

On this _____ day of _____,

The KING'S LAW is approved.

King   _____

Queen   _____

Prince   _____

Prince   _____

Resources

"We are all pilgrims on the same journey but some pilgrims have better road maps"

—*Nelson DeMille*

We all need guidance. It's how we get better. Unfortunately, good advice and sound ideas are sometimes hard to find. The following is a list of websites that may help guide your family through its journey. These resources provide a variety of useful suggestions, up to date information, downloads and links.

I briefly describe the content and focus of each website in the table below. You'll notice that many of the websites overlap, providing alternative resources that cover similar subject matter. I recommend visiting competing websites and selecting those with the features that best suit your needs and personality.

In addition, take some time to surf the net for new sites. The cyber-world evolves very quickly and new websites sprout up all the time. Visit www.yourfamilyconstitution.com to view our most current links.

Online Parenting Resources:	Downloadable Charts	Products for Sale	Online Communities	Links to Other Websites	
Camping and Outdoors					
www.acacamps.org				•	
www.campparents.com				•	
www.gettingoutside.com			•	•	
www.ymca.net			•	•	
Childcare					
www.childcare-ppin.com			•		
Chores & Allowance					
www.chorecharts.com	•			•	
www.freeprintablebehaviorcharts.com	•			•	
www.handipoints.com	•	•	•	•	
www.payjr.com	•			•	
General Parenting Advice					
www.busyparentsonline.com	•		•	•	
www.childdevelopmentinfo.com		•	•	•	
www.familieswithpurpose.com	•	•		•	
www.family.go.com	•	•		•	
www.familyeducation.com	•	•	•	•	
www.familysanitysavers.com				•	
www.familytune.com	•	•		•	
www.funplayfulparent.com	•	•		•	
www.iparenting.com	•	•	•	•	
www.kidsource.com	•	•	•	•	
www.parentingweekly.com	•	•	•	•	
www.pbs.org/parents				•	
Travel					
www.familytravelnetwork.com		•		•	

	Chore and Allowance Ideas	Incentive Ideas	Indoor Activities	Outdoor Activities	Travel Advice and Deals	Household Finance Tools	Health & Safety Information	General Parenting Advice	Divided by Age-Group
				•	•		•		
				•	•				
				•	•			•	
			•	•	•		•	•	
			•					•	
	•	•				•			
	•	•					•	•	•
	•	•	•			•			
	•	•				•			
	•	•	•	•	•	•	•	•	•
		•					•	•	
	•	•	•	•	•	•	•	•	
	•	•	•	•	•	•	•	•	•
		•	•	•	•	•	•	•	•
				•	•	•	•	•	
	•	•	•	•			•	•	
	•	•	•	•	•		•	•	
	•	•	•	•		•	•	•	•
		•	•	•		•	•	•	•
				•		•	•	•	•
			•				•	•	
				•	•				